ALLIES

A PROJECT OF *BOSTON REVIEW'S* ARTS IN SOCIETY PROGRAM

This publication was made possible by generous support from
THE FORD FOUNDATION
THE CAMERON SCHRIER FOUNDATION
VERNON OI

Editors-in-Chief Deborah Chasman & Joshua Cohen

Executive Editor Chloe Fox

Managing Editor and Arts Editor Adam McGee

Senior Editor Matt Lord

Engagement Editor Rosie Gillies

Contributing Editors Junot Díaz, Adom Getachew, Walter Johnson, Robin D. G. Kelley, Lenore Palladino

Contributing Arts Editors Ed Pavlić & Evie Shockley

Editorial Assistants Thayer Anderson & Stijn P. Talloen

Arts in Society Readers Nadia Alexis, Lauren Artiles, Erinn Batykefer, Luca Johnson, Max Lesser, Spencer Quong, Spencer Ruchti, Ben Rutherford, Jacob Sunderlin, Oriana Tang

Marketing and Development Manager Dan Manchon

Finance Manager Anthony DeMusis III

Distributor The MIT Press, Cambridge, Massachusetts, and London, England

Printer Sheridan PA

Board of Advisors Derek Schrier (chairman), Archon Fung, Deborah Fung, Alexandra Robert Gordon, Richard M. Locke, Jeff Mayersohn, Jennifer Moses, Scott Nielsen, Robert Pollin, Rob Reich, Hiram Samel, Kim Malone Scott

Interior Graphic Design Zak Jensen & Alex Camlin

Cover Design Alex Camlin

Allies is *Boston Review* Forum 12 (44.4)

Mark Nowak's "Solidarity Through Poetry" is adapted from *Social Poetics*, forthcoming from Coffee House Press.

Vijay Iyer and Robin D. G. Kelley's "Ally: From Noun to Verb" was recorded and funded by the Octave Music / The Erroll Garner Jazz Project. It was recorded at The Village Studios, with engineering by Brandyn Marko.

To become a member, visit:
bostonreview.net/membership/

For questions about donations and major gifts,
contact: Dan Manchon, dan@bostonreview.net

For questions about memberships, call 877-406-2443
or email Customer_Service@bostonreview.info.

Boston Review
PO Box 425786, Cambridge, MA 02142
617-324-1360

ISSN: 0734-2306 / ISBN: 978-1-946511-49-2

CONTENTS

POETRY

ETC.

EDITORS' NOTE
Adam McGee, Ed Pavlić, & Evie Shockley

IN *ALLIES*, we ask artists how they approach a question that animates many of *Boston Review*'s political essays: How do people who are not alike forge productive alliances? This is not only a political question —all relationships are in some sense acts of bridge-building. But in a moment of global and national chaos fueled in part by intensified identity wars, it feels critical to see if artists have ideas that others have missed.

The result is an anthology rich in insight and complexity. Arranged in an arc that moves from familial, private, erotic, and ecological concerns to explicitly political ones, it blends genres to approach the theme from a plurality of perspectives. We didn't ask anyone to toe a party line, and many among the contributors and editors are skeptical and critical of the term "ally," preferring accomplices, comrades, partners, lovers, family, revolutionaries. . . .

Editing was collaborative. Evie Shockley and Ed Pavlić, Arts in Society's contributing editors, generated lists of authors to invite and helped think through which poems spoke meaningfully to each other. They also helped recruit Ladan Osman, who judged our Annual Poetry Contest, and Yvonne Adhiambo Owuor, our Aura Estrada Short Story Contest judge. Osman and Owuor selected winners as well as finalists, many of which are included here. Each frames the theme in a new light, greatly enriching the issue. The original idea for *Allies* came from Arts Editor Adam McGee, who then also worked to fill in gaps and did hands-on editing, with help from a cohort of readers, assistants, and colleagues.

Allies is the first book produced by the Arts in Society project. Thanks to the generous support of our funders, readers can look forward to a similar themed volume every fall. We hope you'll join us as we explore how the arts speak to the most urgent concerns of our time.

TWO

Sagit Emet, translated from the Hebrew
by Yaron Regev

(a finalist for the Aura Estrada Short Story Contest)

WE WERE ASLEEP going there. We were two. And too ancient. Ten and a half and five and three quarters. That is too old. That is antique. That is considered lost. And it means having no family forever and ever. It means having no home.

We were asleep. It was such a miracle that it made us fall asleep on the road.

That morning, a lot of people came to the boarding school. Volunteers. They wore black T-shirts with a red heart and our boarding school name written in English above, and in Hebrew below: "Matrix ❤ The Children's Village." That was what their shirts read. The volunteers printed them specially, because their workplace is called "Matrix." That was what Clara explained to us. She's the one who takes care of us.

The people in the black T-shirts built stalls on the grass. Cotton candy, and inflatable slides and darts. They played the best music ever. They kept smiling and shouting, "What's up kids? Are we having fun today, or what?"

At first, we just peeked out the window, then we left the room and went outside and did what we had to do—we slid on the slide, and ate pink cotton candy on a stick, and jumped on the trampoline.

And after we ate hot dogs and even more pink cotton candy, we went to take a peek in their SUVs. They were parked by the dining room. Their windows were dark, but when we pressed our faces against them, we could see everything. Those little trees that spread a nice smell hanging from the mirror, coins scattered like gumballs by the driver's seat. We even saw the little chairs fastened with seat belts to the rear seats.

One SUV was open. We found that out after pressing the handle and the door opened. We knew we shouldn't, but we still climbed inside and sat in the little chairs at the back. We folded into them and then it was hard to get up. Which was funny. Chair by chair, we held hands. We thought about what would happen if we fell asleep in the SUV and the owner only found us when he reached his home. But then Clara showed up.

"What are you doing here?" She was furious. "Are you two crazy? Get out right now!"

Then the owner came. He had grey cropped hair, and even though the SUV was his, he wasn't angry at all. He even kept smiling and spoke loudly. "What's up, kids? So, you like cars, eh?" Clara said she was sorry and sent us back to the trampoline.

We saw her whispering with the SUV guy. We saw her crossing her hands. We knew what she was saying, we could read it on her lips: *"Those two! I don't know what will become of them."* That's what she always said. We knew she was acting out the words with those hands she crossed, and with that throaty, Russian accent. *"Those two—they're tight,"* she probably told him. *"Those two—they're always together."* Clara needs her hands to talk for her because nobody understands her Russian, and she doesn't have enough Hebrew words. First, she wipes them on the red robe tied to her hips, then she laces the fingers of one hand into the spaces between the fingers of the other, and then she tightens them together. *"Those two—like Siamese twins!"* Her fingers are like two rakes with their blades tangled. *"We've tried everything with those two."* She must have sighed. *"Everything. First, we separated them . . ."* That was what we imagined her telling the SUV guy, because we've heard her say it before. *"The little one in the little boys' house and the girl in the older girls' house. But the little one ran out to be with her every night, and we had to drag him screaming back to the little boys' house every morning. We even started locking the little boys' house."*

The SUV guy listened and kept saying yes with a nod of his head. We guessed Clara's words. We could imagine her L's, like liquorice melting in spit pools in her mouth.

WE WERE ONLY seven and a half and two and three quarters when we came to the village boarding school. Each put in a separate little house; each with strange children the same age. We lay on the beds and forced ourselves to keep our eyes open so as not to fall asleep, so we wouldn't dream of all the things adults do to children. We heard a door creaking and dreamed of heavy footsteps in the corridor and remembered the smell of bodies, and hair and sweat. Our stomachs were crushed. We couldn't fall asleep.

On the third day, after we found the drawer where they hid the keys in the staff room, they found us together. Fast asleep. Huddling on the same bed. The next night, they hid the key. We banged our fists against the door. We went crazy. We bit Clara. We cried. We cursed. And we ended up winning.

Most people want a cute baby. Doesn't matter if it's white or black, so long as it's a small little baby. The sort that doesn't understand anything. The sort that you can do things to without him talking; do things next to him without his understanding. A baby who knows only what his body knows—burp, sleep, cry, yawn. Most people don't want an older child whose mouth is already dirty. A child who knows how to curse and bite, and steal keys, and wet his bed, and sometimes even stinks it out with smelly poop. What do they need with a kid who pulls scary faces? What do they need with a kid who hisses through his brushed teeth, using dirty words like "son of a bitch," or "motherfucker," or "fuck you and your family"? Do they need a kid like that? They sure don't.

We're not babies anymore. We're just too big. And there's two of us. One's hard enough, so two? There's no way in hell. That's what we heard Clara saying to Nahum with a sigh one day. Then we realized why new kids were coming—old kids had gone, and only we were still here. Oh, and there's Abeba, who's thirteen, and the Leonidov twins, who are also big, and also two. Like us.

Anyway, we were sleeping when we got there. We fell asleep because we were tired of all that fun day of volunteering. And because of the miracle. It was too much for us. In a second, we fainted in the backseat of Nahum's car. We barely managed to see him smiling from the rear-view mirror, saying, "Fasten your seat belts, children," before sleep crawled all over our bodies. We sank into the upholstery, our nostrils filled with the familiar smell of our own bodies. We got high on it. The soft flesh of the stomach, the pursed lips. Cords of spit dripping onto the seat. Body within body, heat within heat. There's a song that goes something like that. The first foster mommy sang it, or was it the second? We can't exactly remember.

We were old. Because there was no chance anyone would ever want us, we heard when they told us a week ago, "You're going to meet parents. You don't have to." We understood the words—*"Parents. Meeting. Don't have to."* But understanding something in your head is worthless. It's like saying ashtray, or ball, or rag. You understand the sounds and that's it. What we mean to say is that you hear them, but the words are just floating in the air. Nothing happens in your body. And nothing happened in ours.

A week ago, Nahum drove us to a shopping mall in another city. He walked with us like he was our dad and we were his children. The sort of children who ran around in the shopping mall telling their mommies and daddies they wanted them to buy them stuff. We walked by the stores holding each other's hands. Hard. The shopping mall had this wonderful smell. And the lights. And all the people there. And the noise.

We wanted to sniff the little soap bars that looked like donuts on a tray. We wanted to put them in our mouths, those little soaps with green and blue leaves frozen inside, like the fossils in the science room. We wanted to bite them. But Nahum told us not to touch and took us straight to the third floor where everyone was eating.

Even before we got there, we knew. We squeezed each other's hands—there they were, the parents we might be having soon, sitting on the McDonald's benches. She had a yellowish face, and he was tall with a bent back. They looked sad, but started smiling when they saw us. Nahum shook the bent man's hand, and the yellowish woman's, who gave him this sad smile. Nahum looked at us through his blue eyes. "Children," he told us, "I'll just leave you here now, all right?"

After Nahum had drifted away a little, the woman asked, "What do you feel like having? Are you hungry?" We shrugged. She tried again. We looked at each other. We had eaten before going to the mall. Still, this was McDonald's. We didn't answer.

"I'll get you something, all right?" She smiled. "And if you don't want it now, they can wrap it up for us to take away." We looked at each other. We spoke with our eyes. She could see our hunger, and that was a good sign, even though we always kept it hidden.

The woman went to order and we sat in front of the tall man with the bent back. He wasn't smiling, but his eyes were as soft as a sponge, and half closed, and tired. He said, "You know this is my first time eating in McDonald's? Can you believe it?"

We looked at each other. "This isn't our first time!" we said immediately. "It's our fourth!"

He was impressed. "Well, thanks to you two, I'm eating here today too," he told us. "What do you say about that?"

It was weird, and we didn't know if we should believe him.

The woman brought us a tray with hamburgers and Cokes and fries, and we stormed at it like our stomachs were empty and not just our thoughts.

Most of the time she was silent and smiling, and looking very confused. She dipped her fries in mayo instead of ketchup. We talked about food and what we liked to eat most in the world. Actually, they asked, and we answered. The daddy told us funny names of funny foods we had never heard about—mamaliga and borscht. It made us laugh.

The mommy had a million questions. "How old are you, Meital?"
"How about you, Ben?"
And—"What subjects do you like most at school?"
And—"Who do you like to play with most in kindergarten?"
And—whether or not we had friends.
And what made us happy.

We answered everything, even though we didn't like it. Too many people were always asking us too many questions. But we answered because they looked kind of miserable with the bent back and the yellowish face. And after we ate all the food, we went to the play area by the McDonald's where they had these slides with mattresses, and you can climb.

At first, they sat on a red sponge bench and looked at us with their sad smiles. Then, the bent-up daddy took off his shoes as well, and climbed and slid with us on the slide. He was the only daddy doing that, and it looked like the yellow mommy liked that, because she couldn't stop laughing and got up from the bench and walked barefoot to the edge of the slide and waited for us and caught us when we slid down. It was as if she was hugging us. We slid again and again, and all over again. It was nice. She had this smell.

Children were waiting in line for the slide, but we pushed past them to slide even more. Until another daddy, short and nervous-looking, went to the bent-back daddy and began to shout. "You should educate your children a little better!" His hand slashed the air. He sent it forward like a sword, as if to say there's a line here!

We spoke with our eyes. The short daddy thought that bent back was our real daddy and that yellow face was our real mommy. It made us feel good all over our bodies.

Just when we were about to leave, Nahum came back and the mommy and daddy asked if we had had fun and if we'd like to meet them again. We said yes. We held hands.

The daddy said, "Thanks to you, not only did I eat in McDonald's, I also slid on the slide!"

The mommy said, "See you soon. I've had so much fun with you." She smiled.

Nahum said, "All right, children, now let's head home."

Saying home is just like saying rag, or ashtray, or ball. It's just sounds. But that day, the sounds made our bodies feel something. Home. We felt it all over our bodies.

That all happened exactly a week ago.

TODAY, after the Matrix people went away and left our grass empty of stalls and trampolines, Nahum called us and said we were going away for the weekend, that we should pack quickly because we'd be leaving in an hour, so we had to hurry up.

We slept the whole way. It was so much of a miracle that it made us fall asleep. Even though it was still light outside.

They have a beautiful house. Real big. With a garden and rooms and everything. "There, you see?" The yellow mommy smiled in the corridor. "You're right next to us. This is Meital's room, and Ben's room is just next door."

We stood behind her holding hands. We spoke with our eyes. We asked if we could sleep together, and she got a little scared. "Sure, of course. I just set this up for you, but you can sleep any old way you're used to."

We didn't go to McDonald's. Even though we kind of hoped we would. The daddy made meatballs. He asked if we wanted to help him make the meatballs and put them in the pot with the red sauce.

We helped him. We were happy the meatballs turned out so nice and round. We wanted him to know we were good kids. That they should definitely take us.

We ate the meatballs with mashed potatoes. Then the daddy asked if we knew how to do long passes with a soccer ball. He had once played soccer for a real professional team. Which was nice.

Every time they asked us a question or suggested something, we looked at each other and spoke with our eyes.

Before going to bed, we watched a movie in the living room. *Frozen*. The mommy laid down on the sofa and we sat on the other side. The daddy was next to her and hugged her. It felt kind of awkward. We looked at the movie, and at the yellow mommy and

Emet

bent-back daddy lying next to each other eating the popcorn they'd made for us. Our eyes kept darting from side to side. On one side Elsa was singing on the television, on the other side was daddy with his tired eyes, and mommy with her yellowish face. The way they were glued to each other on that sofa! The way they lay side by side with the popcorn between them. And love.

We went to sleep like we were used to. In the same room, on the same narrow bed. Real tight. That was why we didn't notice the mommy coming in. Because we were sleeping. But we suddenly heard her whisper, "Oh my, everything is all wet here . . ." She woke us gently. "Come cuties, get up a little moment." She stroked our cheeks.

We stood with our eyes closed and heard her taking new sheets and blankets from the closet. "Maybe you're afraid of sleeping on your own?" she said. "After all, this is a new house," she muttered, as if to herself. Our eyes turned into little slits when she changed our pajamas, but we didn't open them. On purpose. "Maybe you'd like to sleep in our room, eh? What do you say?"

We didn't say anything.

She picked the mattress up from the bed. "Come with me."

We went with her. Wobbling. Through the slits that were our eyes, we saw her spreading the narrow mattress on the floor beside their double bed. Through the slits we heard the daddy waking up. He asked, "What are you doing?"

"Don't worry about it, babe, go back to sleep. Everything's fine," she said. She brought our pillows and blankets from the other room and said to us, "That's it. Now lie down. We're right here next to you. If you need anything—just holler."

Shadows crept up the walls. The daddy snored a little, the mommy didn't.

We listened to the silence. We followed the shadows. And our eyes closed.

There was this smell hanging in the air.

I didn't know if I was allowed to, but I felt I was.

I got up from the mattress. I climbed on top of the double bed and lay in the empty space between the daddy and mommy. She was soft. She had boobies. I heard her breathing.

I pulled up the blanket and pressed the place where I'll have boobies myself one day against her back. I circled her tummy with my hand. I felt it. Soft. Smooth. Just like that word, "Mommy."

"Who's this?" She opened blue eyes that twinkled in the dark and turned her gaze to me, "Meital? Is that you?"

"Yes," I whispered back quietly, and hugged her tummy even tighter. "Yes." I looked through my slits straight into her eyes, "I am me."

Emet

&

Christopher Kempf

Or infinity almost, turned upright. As in
"to sweep & dust & arrange a room

nicely, to wash & iron fine clothes, to cook cakes
& custards & jellies & cut out & make

quite a variety of habiliment," mistress
Tryphena Fox enjoined of her slave girl, Maria. Or "e"

& "t" tightened to a cincture. Calligraphic bow. So signifying
union, perhaps, or contraction. As in Adam

& his affianced at the field's edge, the angel
above them—swept plumage, flaming sword—for all the world

like some hovering monument. Man
    & woman, thenceforth. Or North

    & South, "our sovereignties & feudal arrangements
are leveled to the ground," one Carolina planter

wept of his spoiled pleasure-tract. Who fashioned
    from the rite & manner of the past their protocol

    of empire. Épées & flintlocks at ten paces. The ladies
poised like mastiffs in the drawing room. Decorum

& dominance. The body
    on horseback, for instance—at Manassas

    & Gettysburg, at Charlottesville, of Lee
& Beauregard—reflects,

in its bronze ease, the utter authority
    of bloodline, the fine, affected rhetoric

    so homesick it seems almost
Eden, antebellum Virginia. Mississippi. You remember

the metaphor, yes? The president, March 1861—"a wife & husband
    may pass beyond the reach of one another, but the different parts

Kempf

of a country cannot." Or nation
as doomed beloveds, say— Shut up

in fevered scriptoria, tenth-century monks
   married one letter to the next

   in their painstaking crib-work, one's speed
& economy being, for them, the exactest augury

of righteousness. Described the coiled glyph
   as *ligature*. As in

"to bind or fasten." "To flirt." From the hipbone's
bondage & pliancy. The premise—everything

attaches. The twelve-year-old—Ohio, orange tip
   missing from the airsoft replica—lead-

mangled in his playground gazebo leads south sooner
or later, we know, to the seized runaway bucked

& gagged in the courtyard dust. Instructed
   to sit, a slave drew his knees to chest then, the leg

   of a table placed beneath his kneecaps, wrists
wrapped around shinbones, bit down

on the overseer's choke-rag. As in— &. Or
    bind rune. Relic insignia. Sigil. Or consider

    a competing account— How, healed
of their motley afflictions—of impotence

often, of gout & pertussis & dog bites—visitants lifted themselves
    like saints from the springs at Gettysburg, emblems,

    the papers reported, "of national deliverance
& regeneration." & praise

Jesus. What people
    is not the undying aspiration of juncture? To one—

astrological imprint. Another—
a rope wound over itself like a lasso, like

a knot or noose. "Our needles now
    are our weapons," Confederate war bride

    Lucy Butler pencils in her diary
May 24, 1861. Or "ice cream

in summer & oysters in winter" one freedman,
    Owen Robinson, remembered peddling

for tourists in the war's wake. As in praline
& lemon. As in Malpeques

& Flats & Kumamotos. Bluepoints. Olympias
   & Beausoleils. The tin tray

   sweating with its bounty. The bed of ice—Owen
having crushed it by hand, having

shucked the hinged things himself—
   like diamonds.

TO THE FORDHAM
Samuel R. Delany

NEWT WAS NOT a little man. He was thick, hairy, and hulking, and after an astonishing experiment at seven, which had left him confused for almost eight months before he tried it again, by the age of eleven, he was jerking off between three and five times a day.

Thirty-four years later, Newt—in New York City for almost seven months—had been riding the subway end to end for almost three months, during which time he had not had a shower and, for two weeks, had had no shoes.

Most of the day, he'd been sleeping, till he got hungry. Then he'd come out and try to panhandle up some food, but that was a few hours off. And he'd managed to find somewhere to beat his meat between five and eight times a day. He'd done it between the cars, about an hour ago; it had run down the far side of the door, and he'd returned to sit down to drift off again almost immediately.

When he blinked, a dark-haired kid—seventeen? eighteen?—was sitting across the car from him, beside a backpack. Newt opened his eyes a crack, saw the kid was bending forward and, unlacing first his left sneaker, then his right, fingered them free of his feet, sat up with both of them hooked to one hand, and shoveled them into the backpack. Barefoot, the kid stood up, unbuckled a wide leather belt, thumbed apart the button, unzipped his fly, and dropped the pants (from the rivets and the change pocket, Newt realized they were black jeans; his own were a pair of green workpants, with some white and orange paint stains, he'd found in a trash receptacle, which someone had left and gratefully he had taken), awkwardly stepped out of them, pushed down a pair of black briefs with "FELLINI" in broad white letters, slipped them down over his knees, and, hopping on one foot, then the other, got out of those as well. The briefs were set on the knapsack; the jeans were pulled up and buckled. He sat once more and shoved his briefs into the sack after his shoes.

Newt glanced to the near, then the far end of the subway car. They were the only two on it. The kid had not been circumcised, and Newt felt himself shifting inside his own pants. This wasn't going to be some sort of absurd sex dream of the kind that had occasionally bewildered him during his 124 weeks in Leavenworth out in Kansas—that was almost 15 years ago. Since then he had managed to get to Miami's Biscayne Blvd. and three other cities, all of which had Market Streets, one of which was San Francisco, one of which was Philadelphia, before he'd ended up in New York. He moved one foot an inch over on the gritty subway flooring. A couple of shadows from the beams outside the elevated train streaked through the car. No, this wasn't a dream. At least he was pretty sure it wasn't.

He closed his eyes, then slitted them enough to look around the car once more. The train was coming to a stop. The doors to the left of the kid opened, and nobody got on. Newt opened his eyes and glanced down at his stained pants. It wasn't all just paint; there was a lot of dried semen left over from a project he'd thought about perhaps a month ago, when it had occurred to him that that might be a way to get somebody's attention, till finally he'd decided he was probably just too old and not the sort that anybody was really going to go after the way sometimes it had happened in jail or, since then, a few times when he'd been managing to get between here and there—wherever "there" happened to be. Newt lifted his big hand to his mouth and began to gnaw on his thumbnail.

The boy was blinking, staring . . . which is when it hit Newt that in getting rid of his shoes and underpants (and the kid had not zipped his fly), the kid was . . . imitating him!

Newt was confused—but not stupid. He had been a bum long enough to learn that some guys, yeah, liked to blow him, which, if they had some dirty pictures or something, he could get into. But the habit of owning nothing had eclipsed any habits of buying himself extras of any sort, especially disposable ones that were so ephemeral and expensive. He opened his eyes and frowned.

Across from him, the kid swallowed.

Without moving, Newt said over the mechanical thunder that started up again with the train: "You want something?"

The kid blinked, shrugged, looked sheepish. . . .

Newt smiled. "Come on over here—if you want."

Delany

Without even looking, the kid grabbed his knapsack and was across the aisle between them to sit beside Newt, who was still gnawing.

Newt looked toward the far door between the cars again and put his arm around the kid's shoulder. He squeezed in what he hoped was a friendly way, though he was somewhat frightened. He was not sure of what. He'd done enough weird things in his life, but he also felt too tired and disoriented to get kicked off a train right then. So far, though, there'd been no sign of a conductor to put them out. He frowned back at the kid beside him, who was not looking at his face: Of course, he was staring down at Newt's half-gaping fly.

"Hey—wha' do you *like* me or somethin'?"

The kid said loudly but with no inflection: "Yeah . . ."

"Ya wanna suck my dick—or somethin'?"

Still without looking up, the kid nodded.

Looking down, Newt realized the kid was grinning; or was he about to cry . . . ?

"Yeah. . . !" The kid's face came up. It was a grin in a face somewhat unshaven, which made Newt wonder if he wasn't older than Newt had first thought. "I wish you had some pictures or somethin'."

Immediately, the kid pulled his sack into his lap and went in with one hand and tugged out two magazines with colorful photographic covers.

"I'll be honest—" Newt chuckled—"I prefer the ones with the women." On the cover of the top one was a curvaceous, large-breasted, and wholly uninteresting blonde. Again, Newt frowned. "I mean, I guess, you know . . . darker ones." He shrugged.

The kid pulled the magazine behind the first out and put it on top. "Like this?"

With a falling inflection, Newt said: "You got everything, don'cha?" Then he frowned and started gnawing again. The women pictured were not only black, he realized, but she-males. During that nebulous time of experimentation right after release from his second and last term in prison, he'd had intimate friendships with Alyse (four years his senior) and Ginger, but even though, up until a few years ago, he'd still sent Ginger the occasional postcard—the only person he'd ever sent postcards to—he hadn't had actual sex with either.

He hadn't had sex with anyone, really, except guys. He just wasn't used to them being younger than he was. That was really confusing.

The kid put the two magazines back and pulled out a third—*Dark Surprise!* Newt felt the kid's foot up against his own and lifted his enough for the kid's to slide under and pushed his own down. That seemed to have settled something, though he was not exactly sure what. "Does that feel good?"

The kid said: "We can do it here if you want. I don't think nothin's gonna happen, but we should really get off and go into the john if you wanna get serious." He did not pull his foot from under Newt's.

Newt took the magazine with his free hand and looked at it without settling it into his lap. The kid let the knapsack fall over onto the seat, and his other hand was underneath it, slipping into Newt's zipper-less fly, where, beneath the kid's fingers, Newt felt himself stiffening.

"If that's what you're looking for, man, I'll suck you off right now. But next stop's Fordham. There's a good movie house right down the block from the station. We could go in there and nobody'd care if we fooled around."

By the time we left the movie, I knew Newt didn't know how to read. He wanted me to read the words at the head of the movie and was surprised to learn it was the title and the names of the stars, the producers, and the director. He said he'd always wondered how people found out the names of movies and TV shows and things like that.

Newt had been living with me for three months, and whenever he thought I was even vaguely horny, he'd lie down on the rug or the couch and beckon me to get down on top of him.

"Man, that day on the subway, when we first went to that theater, whatever the fuck its name was—"

"The Fordham—"

"—I never figured you had your own place. I lived with my dad right up to that time the police come dragged me to Leavenworth. I know that's in Kansas, but I still don't know what state we was in before that. And I ain't never had my own place in my life."

(It took me a week of him coming by my place every day to bring me half the money he'd made panhandling to learn not only that, while he could copy down someone's address, he didn't really read; he didn't know what state his father had raised him in, or what his last name was, and that he'd learned how to jerk off by sitting on his father's lap in their cabin while the old man brought himself to orgasm—but no he wasn't particularly eager to find out where he was or if he was alive. He'd eaten better since he'd left, but hadn't learned much of anything at all. I also knew his jail nickname had been Newt the Brute, which was the biggest joke I think I ever heard. But in jail they hadn't thought so.)

Allies

I grinned and got down on my knees and lay down on top of him.
I got my dick out of my fly and into his that was still broken and began
rubbing—that man was always hard and ready to have me rub off on
him. He wrapped both arms around me, then released one, brought his
hand up to his mouth, and began to gnaw on his nails.

Newt opened the magazine at random—and, wouldn't you
know, there was a nude picture of a black woman who actually
looked like Alyse, a little, but after a roll-and-tuck job. "They
actually do stuff in movie houses up here? Somebody said somethin' about that to me when I was hitchin' in, but I thought they
were kiddin'."

"Other than the Fordham up here in the Bronx, just some of
the places down on Eighth Avenue—somebody told me there were
two out in Brooklyn I've never visited. This Turkish exhibitionist
brought me up here once, and it was actually pretty kicky. I've been
there three or four times, and nothing bad ever happens. It's not as
hot as the Eighth Avenue ones, but it's better than nothin'."

"You mean like a peep show?"

"No, it's a movie. You don't have to stick your dick through no
glory hole—except in the basement john, between the stalls. . . . If
that's what turns you on."

"No kidding . . ." Newt was surprised. With three-quarters of
a year in New York, he hadn't been to any movies at all yet. "Well,
I don't got no money."

"If you want to fuck around for an afternoon, I'll pay for us
goin' in, get us a couple of sandwiches, or some sodas or some beer
if that's what you want . . . ?"

Delany

"Hey, I ain't been to a movie since . . . ?" Had he been in a movie since there'd been those movie nights, back in jail on Fridays back in Leavenworth?

"It's the Fordham. There's a deli at the end of the block."

"Nobody's gonna mind if we do shit . . . ?"

"It's dark in there," the kid said. "Besides, that's what everybody's doin' in there."

Newt found himself intrigued. "Well, okay . . ." It sounded like something he wanted to see.

The train was slowing.

The kid stood and hooked his knapsack by one strap.

They pulled into the station, stopped, and the door pulled back. (When you had doors like that in a house, Newt thought, they called them pocket doors, but in a subway they were just sliding doors.) He followed the kid out to the platform. "You in school someplace?"

"Naw," the kid said. "I got a job. Down on Forty-Seventh Street."

Since there was no one around, they pushed out the swinging gates beside the stile and past the change booth, then started out and down the steps.

Newt reached into his broken fly and tugged out his cock. "I'm glad you like this thing so much."

"Yeah," the kid said. "Are you an exhibitionist? The Turkish guy who first brought me up here after I met him in one of the places downtown hangs out in the Fordham. He likes to wave his meat around like that. He says it gives him a hard-on. What kind of a sandwich you want? The pastrami's pretty good. There's not a lot of people out on the street up here, but you should probably put your pen in your pocket until we get inside."

"Huh? What—? Oh."

"I wanna get a chance to suck on it, and I don't want you to get in no trouble before we get in."

"Hey, you're a good guy."

The kid laughed. "Naw, I'm just fuckin' horny."

"Hey, how do *you* get off?"

"If we can sit in the front, I can hump your leg like a dog. You stick your fingers into my mouth or something, and I'll shoot."

Newt chuckled. "My dog used to do that when I was a kid at home. I could even get off on that. I wonder if I could still get off that way with you."

The kid said, "Hey, as long as, you know—you give me somethin' to suck on. Like, you know . . . your fingers."

Newt laughed, raised his thick hand to his mouth. "My fingers . . . ?" He took his hand down and looked at it, then began to gnaw again. "Yeah, I bite my nails all to shit. My dad and my teachers used to tell me forever I gotta stop that."

The kid said, "Probably if you had, I wouldn't have sat down across from you."

"Shit . . ." Newt said, again surprised.

"Come on," the kid said. "Put your dick away."

"Oh, yeah . . ." Newt slid his cock back within his broken fly. Three more steps and they walked onto the pavement, warm in the sunlight. Again, surprisingly, the kid put his foot down on top of Newt's. Newt looked up at him, stopping.

Delany

"You walk around the city barefoot, and everybody just thinks you're crazy. It's a good way to get left alone."

"Yeah?" Yet again Newt chuckled. "Well, maybe whoever told you that was right. Hey, I hope you got another subway token so when we finish, I can get back on the subway."

"Don't worry," the kid said. "I got you taken care of."

"Well, show me this theater."

Without saying anything, the kid started walking again.

At the street's end, a sign—"FORDHAM"—hung down the upper stories of the building to the top of the marquee. Underneath they could see the bulbs that were on even in the warm July morning.

A couple of weeks later, they went to the end of the Fiftieth Street subway station and, with the kid's iPhone, made some porn videos of Newt jerking off in the station and coming on the grating up against the tiled wall (the kid had a three-day-a-week part-time job at a warehouse on the edge of Marble Hill), which they sold on PornHub for $25 a piece, though PornHub asked them to remake them so that you couldn't see Newt's face, though Newt said he didn't mind. A few months later, they sold some more and only curbed it when Newt's income started to be high enough that they had to think about taxes.

—June 24, 2019
Philadelphia

WHEN THE CLIMATE CHANGED
Samuel R. Delany

THE NEWS ON THE COMPUTER was full of the damage from the six tornadoes to the south, and the forest fires were less than two hundred miles away. He wanted to have sex, mad, passionate sex of the sort he had had last week through his Tinder app, and he knew with whom and where to find them.

But it was just too hot.

FROM THE KINDREDS

Meredith Stricker

(*a* Boston Review *Annual Poetry Contest finalist*)

"Selves are signs. Lives are thoughts. Semiosis is alive."

"And the world is thus animate."

"We, in short, are not the only kinds of *we*."

—Eduardo Kohn, *How Forests Think: Toward an Anthropology*
Beyond the Human

dear Animate:

We were talking about the difference between "kin" and "kindred"—
blood relation vs. connection not strictly defined by family. Kin can
narrow to claustrophobic ritual and feuds, while kinship intermingles
and crosses blood lines. How large is "family" or "kinship"?
Can kin include those outside our family, our species?
Who includes us, who do we include? trees with their oxygen
out-breath? bees? those who remain stateless, undocumented or illegal?

the "inanimate"—rocks and rivers? What happens to a culture
that narrows and nuclears its sense of family?

Cecilia Vicuña says "in her performance Theresa Cha would give
the audience white cards that read 'distant relative'.
Rocks, water, fire are also our relatives."

dear distant. dear relative

we are the shadows of
our animals

The brightness of the animal

"embedded in the visible that hides them"
—Jean-Christophe Bailly

> there was the flaring
> of bodies in sun's path the brightness
> of an awkward and prehistoric body
> with wide-sieved mouth, wider than Jerusalem
> pelican folded like a dark arrow plunges
> without hesitation into the abode of water
> 60,000 pelicans once sheltered in Gulf rookeries
> now thousands of dead birds
> the young emaciated and abandoned

Stricker

to the spreading sheen of oil
dense with dispersants
water silver-black as feldspar
waves like rapid eye movements
in waters fat and rancid
oil slick unfurls like silk
born pre-erased
crabs born blind
scrambled genetic
the young with
wings pressed back, useless
our industry, our tourists
sores on their skin
mouths wide open
bright words bright day
bright orchard bright water
bright boat bright cloud

—

do you swim with full intelligence
gleaned in intricacies of water
are you more or are you less sentient than whales
do you hear them laid out and skinned against the bow of oblivion
hunted and plundered then rendered
yet still curious about us

—

        in search of the sublime
          many suburbanites
across time zones
      all the tidepools
    hexagonal shapes like beehive cells
       tarry sprawl
              the awe spread and spread our fault line
   where you left me in cold fathomless

When rivers are granted personhood

do corporations dream in clear calm morning
threaded by contrails

   —

if a corporation is a person but not a migrant
does the corporation have a soul but not

the chicken I eat nor the river downstream
from the person of the corporation

if a corporation is a person does it wake up
in dread sometimes like a person does

Stricker

and cannot get up out of its chair unassisted
when its legs no longer work so well its eyes no longer see

the corporation falls down goes to its first day of class
trembling with excitement and terror it gets depressed

gets a pink slip a tumor it is sad it is compassionate
it lies on the ground ecstatic seeing a young pine tree

and one day it lies down on the ground and gives
its body back to the vast, undocumented microbial ferment

breaking down into particles of lyric

—

the sentence, ~~a sentence~~ — a sentience

———

   NOTES:

"The brightness of the animal"

"embedded in the visible . . ." —Jean-Christophe Bailly, *The Animal Side*

"the young emaciated" refers to rookeries of brown pelicans on Raccoon Island in the Gulf after the BP
   oil spill, *National Geographic*, 2010; see "5 Years After BP Oil Spill, Effects Linger and Recovery is Slow,"
   Debbie Elliot, NPR, 2015

"When rivers are granted personhood"

   for title, see "The Legal Personality of Rivers," EMA blog from
   http://www.emahumanrights.org/2019/01/16/the-legal-personality-of-rivers/

"the sentence, a sentence": Ingeborg Bachmann, *Darkness Spoken*

FROM MASS EXTINCTION
Sarah Vap

Nothing that interesting has come out

from inside of us. Nothing worth hurting anything else for.

How life became an endless, terrible competition.

How you say you are a friend to women and girls,

for example, but leave them to deal with it. How you say you could
be a friend to an animal, or a grove

of communicating aspens, but you leave them to deal with it.

How life became an endless, terrible competition.

What should we do with the alphas. What should we do

with all the winners. Turn our backs on them, and my naiveté humiliates me still.

How to subdue the genome that makes us feel dissatisfied, like we need to go get something or kill something.

Like we need to discover something. Or climb to the top of our field. Like we need to make someone do something we want them to do.

Or, the ways in which we stop something better from happening

because it will probably make us look mediocre.

Let's be honest, when we say *ally* or *friend* or *understand*, we really mean we'll be a second in your duel,

but mostly, we'll watch you struggle for your life at a shorter distance than most.

We mean we'll watch you struggle for your life, from close-up. We mean we'll stare at you,

while you're destroyed, and say "that is life."

What do we want from animals. What do we want from watersheds.
What do we want from ecosystems. What do we think is the limit
of what is ours,

and the limit of what is "life" or "our life."

Do you happen to wield the lethal blade of momentum.

Do you happen to worship the upward-turning curve. Do you happen
to hold some kind of rein
in your hand, and do you use it to do something self-protective and
mediocre.

The associative human mind,

replaced with the bureaucratic or the mathematic mind—what number
would you need to hear to be a friend to an ecosystem.

What number do you need to hear. How many wins do you need.

What kind of prestige, or influence, will you hold out for, before you
are a friend to a mountain.

What do you need, in order to stop distinguishing between what
you think is *living*

Vap

and what you think is *not living*.

Think about all of your own systems. Think about how you hold them up over the world,

then drop them, crashing, down on it.

That mountain is covered in snow. It is so beautiful. Is there a fetus inside of it.

Very few things desire human love. How exactly should we *love*

or *be a friend* to that mountain.

We open a mine, and we take what we want out of it, and my sarcasm cuts me still.

ALL WE REMEMBER WILL BE FORGOTTEN
JR Fenn

"It will be the most wonderful sound I could ever imagine, a sound that makes me feel like a fountain, or a wellspring."

—Ted Chiang, "Story of Your Life"

THE EARLIEST SIGHTING was in Reykjavík, beyond the Hallgrím-skirkja at the head of Skólavörðustígur, three hives having been introduced to Iceland in the nineteenth century by missionaries who wished to bring God's bounty to a cold and sparsely peopled land. In chisel-hollowed stumps and backyard boxes, the bees had lived and gathered pollen and spun food and refused to reproduce, their ranks augmented by foreign stocks. In the first of the appearances, the swarms gathered in dark clouds beyond the steam hills, first a smudge on the landscape and then, approaching, taking on shapes—hundred-foot women, their arms reeling wheels in the sky, lurching toward human habitation.

After this they were seen in other locations: near a collection of huts in Mongolia, tenant farmers circled around a fire sharing cups of milk, the creature whirling up out of the darkness of the plain like a dust storm sweeping across the grassland. Appearances were reported outside a village near Fukushima and in the refugee camps of South Sudan, aid workers scrambling to replace the tents whose roofs had been ripped by the great wind of the giant's passing into empty, stargazing holes.

At times they seemed unaware of the presence of humans, as if they could not see the waves of screamers scattering at their feet. At other times they seemed to wish to communicate. There was, for instance, the rented accommodation in Joshua Tree, vacationers standing at the edge of the fenced yard beside a churning, empty hot tub to peer in the direction of a nighttime sound over the hill, the motion sensor light of the neighbor's house switching on, the giant head appearing above the cacti under the pale disc of the moon, rising and rising into a female shape that held her arms before her in what struck the people on the ground below as some strange, choked signature of grief.

Their name emerged as a result of what each one left behind her. Amid the rubble of Eibingen Abbey, on top of and between the strewn and chewed-up concrete blocks of the pylons for the funicular to the Genting Highlands above Kuala Lumpur, beside the esplanade along the Brahmaputra River where it flowed past Guwahati's newly beautified shore—there would be, after her going, small flecks of darkness, iridescent wings and dismembered thoracic sections, spiderwebs of legs too infinitesimal to be seen, in a powdery dust that seemed as though it had been strewn by a careless hand in a collection of rustling, empty carapace parts over the ground, and here and there could be found, too, whole specimens lying on their backs with their legs curled to their stomachs, multi-sectioned eyes blind and upward-looking: the remnants and scattered bodies of bees.

The mothers, people called them, before they knelt to gather specimen after specimen the mothers had left behind, specks in their hands, which they put into boxes to keep in their desks or kitchens, or to send to experts who might know why bees would behave in such a way, taking the shape of women and wandering the land.

And that is how many of these specimens made their way to me.

AT THE TIME, I was becoming aware of my first pregnancy. There had been the loss of appetite—one long, dizzy shiver as I tagged my catches in the cold, metallic air of the high Wuksachi Range, where Muir once wandered. Just before Roland called with the news of the first of the specimens' arrivals, the greatness of the valley had stretched below me in stone cliffs and space plummeting down to the trickle glint of a river half covered by a carpet of trees—I had gasped and leaned against my silver-haired assistant, Jean, under a hollow mountain hemlock, above the tree line. I smelled the powder detergent on Jean's soft shirt, the warmth of his body underneath. The hemlock made a gnarled and dark and cave-like canopy in a clearing of whitebark pines.

I had located, in this clearing, a healthy colony during my year of field work, the bees unaffected by the changes that, I understood later, would usher the mothers into being. Some of the precedents had been sent to my Los Angeles lab already: odd-acting bees, harbingers of the giant walkers. Some of them I had seen for myself, in the Sierras. Some of the bees there had grown listless, and others more aggressive, as though uncomfortable in their roles. I had seen a drone perform a segment of the mating dance, a performance reserved exclusively for queens, moving in an ancient pattern over the heads of the *Achillea millefolium* and attracting the notice of the other drones in the neighborhood. I had seen a queen wander far from her hive, as though she had forgotten her proper home.

Others had been sent to my attention with scribbled notes attached, on which scientists and bee enthusiasts had recorded the details of the odd behaviors. *Drone with queen mandibular pheromone,* a colleague in Beijing wrote, *(E)-9-Oxodec-2-enoic with carboxylic acids and aromatic HOB present in high quantities.* From a bee habitat activist in western New York: *I saw these three bees fly purposefully into the eye of my grandson Bobby, I believe they're trying to tell us what we're too dumb to see.* From a well-known, reclusive apiarist on New Zealand's Stewart Island, *My bees (I enclose samples) have stopped consuming manuka, can you advise me how to get them to eat and pollinate?*

But I had been focused on proving my discovery at the time, tagging all the Sierra bees I could to track their foraging patterns, transporting the healthiest ones and their foods back to the lab, to prove the discovery that had so recently earned me international fame—the Bee Woman, they called me, so often the words rose up as if from a thousand stinging mouths into the soundscape of my dreams.

Roland called as Jean and I were tagging a drone, the two of us crouched close together under a bitter cherry in a small patch of sun. Jean held the stunned drone with the gentlest pinch of his tweezers as I worked to accomplish the tagging with the help of the portable magnifying glass, which we'd arranged on a flat rock where it wobbled back and forth on its unreliable legs, making it harder to see the drone's fragile, threadlike upper femur in order to affix the tag. The phone buzzed in my pocket as I began to wrap the microwire in place below the coxa, buzzed some more and went to messages.

"Come back," Roland said, his voice crackling in the recording. "There is something you will want to see." On the long drive back to Los Angeles, Jean sat in the passenger seat. A former environmental minister for the French government, he'd joined our project three years ago in Rouen. We had been close from the time we crouched in the cow field and I discovered what would garner such acclaim, and bring us all—Roland, Jean, the entire lab—from France to California.

I opened my window as I drove, the leather of the seats too hot. "I've been sick," I said, as the rutted fields passed by, the wind a roar in my left ear.

We passed lone gas stations, white plastic tunnels of strawberry farms in rows. Jean draped the warmth of his hand near my leg, in the well between our seats, as he sat looking out the window at the dust going by. He began to tell me the story of a wolf cub he'd found as a child, the discovery of which had turned his eyes from religion to science, according to the account he gave.

"It was in the back woods, near the stone where my village used to leave the children. Exposure, *expositio*, it was called." His hair was silver white, his skin a plum tan, his face blocky and kind, heading toward death as it was. "It would follow me and lick me," he said, and laughed. "Imagine that, abandoning your pup to human mercy."

As we ventured into the outskirts of the city, tight brown hills and viral sprawl of buildings, we grew silent.

My lab was in northeast Los Angeles, in Glassell Park. When we'd passed the Guatemalan consulate and the bare hills of the canyon nature reserve, after we'd pulled into my designated spot and entered the mirrored glass front of the low white concrete building, Roland met us in the radiant silence of the lobby with a box held out in his hand. He poured its contents onto my fingers, and so the body of a mother specimen first skittered onto my skin, as I felt a wave of nausea push up from the very bottom of my stomach to fill my chest and throat.

I ran to the bathroom, where I dry heaved over the bowl, and then I warmed the first of the mother specimens—still somehow clutched in my hand—to life, on a glass plate under the globular heat lamp, where she lay immobile and then proceeded to drag herself, front foot by front foot, soft and slow, across the pink of the reflective mirror, where I looked down and saw my face as she pulled her body across it, my mouth open with redness, with the stupefied, somewhat transfixed wonder of the human race.

I lifted her in a clear tube and transported her to the old aquarium on the metal table at the back of the lab, which I had created as a habitat for the still-living odd behavers people had sent from around the world. The ones I could not revive went to the freezer graveyard—a box in the laboratory's walk-in cold storage room, placed on the deep bottom shelf on an otherwise empty rack at the rear of the chamber.

"Why do you tend to them?" Roland asked of the aquarium colony.

"I don't know," I said, as more arrived and were revived or sent to the freezer—as the survivors in the aquarium became a shining, penny-burnished ball, which pulsed from within with ragtag, cross-species communication.

And that is how I created the Los Angeles colony.

AS THE NEWS REPORTS poured in, with bumpy footage of mothers rampaging through towns and cities all around the world, I sat by the aquarium and watched the mother specimens crawl through the lacy plastic of soda rings and the remains of a soccer ball—a half-crushed, Bauhaus-style, many-windowed sphere.

The lab also contained an artificial Sierra habitat, thriving with my healthy high-altitude catches, which constituted proof of my discovery, my entire life of research up to that point. Throughout the day, Roland went in and out of its netted door, bringing fresh plants and water. He put the sun lamps on a timer after I began to forget to turn them on.

"Come home, eat," he said. It had been a little while, after the first of the mother specimens arrived, before I had thought to tell him what was stirring inside me. The flutter far down in my abdomen, deep under my heart, the culmination of what we had both thought to be an old, impossible longing.

I was forty-one, we had been trying for years, and of course there had been the invitations that followed the presentation of my discovery, the move to be near the Sierra alpine meadows which had evolved, due to their remoteness, a superior interrelation of flowers and bees.

When I told him, I touched my hand to the cherry red of his cheek and all the bees in the aquarium buzzed noisily beside me. He picked me up and spun me around, then dropped to his knees and sang a French lullaby against my belly the way his mother had once sung to him in Rouen. We had met at his field station there ten years before, after I'd finished my graduate work in Austin. I'd gone on a grant and partnered with his lab, and three years later we were married in Paris, surrounded by flying buttresses and blue-latticed windows, on the steps of Abbot Suger's Saint-Denis. Now we lived in a wooded bungalow in Silver Lake, all shadows and polished floors and recessed windows looking out at evergreens.

It was Jean, though, not Roland, who was present at the moment of my discovery. A Eureka moment, Archimedes in the bathtub, the sort of singular event to which chroniclers return in order to perpetuate the false notion of invention's simplicity. We lay in a field outside of Montigny, near the Forêt Domaniale de Roumare. It was a hot day. The sun made a blazing cavern of the sky and the ground pressed up into our bodies with the dry insistence of a rainless week. We lay close on our stomachs and I could feel Jean's heat through the ground. We lay in the sticky silence of milk-sap shrubs and new larch as we watched a honeybee stumble on her path through short-grown barbs of yellow grass.

She was a European dark bee, and feral, from one of the last pure colonies of *Apis mellifera mellifera* in France. She found a low stalk of aquilegia, its long petals open in a burst of invitation.

And I saw, as though in a flash, some shared design between bee and flower, as the bee's mandible touched itself to the mound of the columbine pistil. I had, during the decade in Rouen that followed my eight years of doctoral work in Austin, been sequencing the DNA of *Apis mellifera mellifera* and the Breton *abeille noire d'Ouessant*, in the subregion of the genome that governs social behavior, which stands as an analogue to that subregion in the flower genome, and in the human genome, too, for that matter.

I believed, at that moment in the field, in some genetic communication taking place in that subregion between the dark bee and the aquilegia, and a particular base pair sprang to mind in visual form.

Intuition is a wonderful and terrible thing, a foreknowledge that frightens in its accuracy.

I found, when I sequenced the DNA of bee and plant together, a mirroring effect in this base pair. An evolved degree of communication, in the material shape of those infinitesimal proteins, a communication that might be enhanced by editing to increase similarity.

I called my discovery sympathy. The ramifications were significant—a genetic basis for the behavioral and morphological connections between bees and plants, a location and physical substrate for symbiosis across organisms.

I conducted my experiments in the Sierra bees, who exhibited the highest degree of genetic mirroring with their flowers. When I edited the base pairs to better reflect one another, I found the changes enhanced advantageous dependency.

Fenn

In the glass-fronted room where Roland now came and went were the bees I had brought back from the healthy Sierra colony up on the mountain, along with the plants on which they fed, the *Ribes roezlii* and *Spiraea densiflora*, the entire habitat thriving due to genetic enhancements I'd made in both bees and flowers. The habitat stood as a web of genetic interdependence, bees and plants bent to one another's benefit at the deoxyribonucleic level. The bees lazed from flower to flower, fat and unconcerned, honey overflowing in great wax chambers. Gooseberry and meadowsweet burst with growth and buds, as if the bees' touch reminded them of their worth. The fruition of my theory was there for all to see—the foundation of interspecies adaptation.

BUT AS THE MOTHER SPECIMENS arrived, and as my belly grew, I turned my back on this glorious habitat. Month by month, I sat and watched the resurrected bees group and separate in their aquarium. There was something about their behavior I could not quite understand, something about their social organization that struck me as unique.

I pressed my forehead to the glass and felt the heat of it on my skin. There was a beautiful kind of buzzing from the grouping of bees within, a plaintive and coherent buzzing that filled my ears and my head, as though this subsonic buzzing might be filling me with a question.

At night when everyone had gone, when Roland had hugged me and run his hands over my growing belly, when he'd told me he'd have dinner waiting in the oven, I stayed beside the aquarium and listened to the colony. Outside the windows, I could see the lights of the city, its buildings and the strangeness of traffic, and on these nights all of this felt extremely far away. It was me and the bees and a new kind of joy, the joy of what was growing within me. I would climb on the metal table and pull up my shirt and slather cold gel on my belly. I had a sonogram for visualizing the interiors of hives, and I'd press the transducer against my skin. I knew that what was growing was not a child yet—I was a scientist above all else—but as I watched her move her arms and legs, I was seized with a welcoming in my being. It seemed, as well, that the bees were aware of my brooding love, and their buzzing grew louder with my anticipation.

"I am growing something inside me, what will be a child," I whispered to the mother colony as my belly grew larger and larger, as I began to sense from within the being I would introduce to all I loved.

And the mother colony whispered back the high whine of their honey-mouthed blessings.

After I lost her, I rarely left the lab. Roland would try, and he even sent Jean, who clung to me with the tenderness of an older man. But I didn't care about any of them, I couldn't listen to anyone's advice. I visited her body many times during the days and nights, her body I had birthed at almost seven months, this fragile and perfect and fully formed being whom I could only think of as my daughter. After I held her and would not let her go, after she arrived in the corner of the bathroom where I crouched as the pain seized me fast, after I'd screamed away the circle of concerned faces that blanched too sick and close—after her skin had grown plastic to the touch, I pulled my skirt over my bloody legs and carried her through the lab to the cold storage room, where I made a cushion with a blackout cloth and placed her on her own on a shelf at the back.

"We need a funeral," Roland said. He had researched it on the Internet. "People have funerals for things like this." He couldn't bring himself to say her name.

"Cassandra," I would say when I visited her. I wouldn't hear of anyone taking her away. I'd arranged her on her stomach, her tiny fingers clasped together, her head at rest and turned so I could see her chin and her bud of a mouth. Her legs I folded gently and tucked up underneath her rump, which curled soft and plump the way a real baby's does. She was so cold, so beautiful, so frozen into crystalline perfection, I could hardly stand the fact that I had made her. I couldn't reconcile myself to the accident that she'd been born so still and quiet, when I'd known her so alive within me.

BY THIS POINT I had begun to change, of course. I sat and watched the bees in their aquarium, watched how they flocked and gathered. The Los Angeles colony, these leavings of the mothers, becoming their own distinct organism.

I leaned my forehead against the glass, and I felt the bees buzzing like a buzzing in my brain. It felt like a tickle deep in my skull, back in the top left quadrant of my cranium. It was there that I had bored the tiny hole, inserted the micropipette with its burden.

I had gone to my child, curled and perfect in the cold room, to take back some of what I'd created. I drilled into her body and cut out a part of one of her ovaries, a tender pink-white cluster of my daughter. From the eggs inside the ovary I extracted her DNA, and from the DNA I extracted the base pair for sympathy. I harvested the eggs to host the DNA from the honeycomb in the Sierra habitat, the only bees in the lab that were reproducing. But I replaced their DNA with DNA from the Los Angeles bees, with my daughter's base pair spliced into the correct groove. I had only mapped the DNA for editing the base pair with which I'd been working—the base pair in which sympathy is housed.

The DNA from the Los Angeles bees with the sympathy base pair from my daughter I inserted into the Sierra eggs. Many Sierra eggs died this way, brown and clustered in their dish, but in the end I gazed down into a clutch of pearly white hosts suspended in translucent purple gel. I took the drill I'd pushed into Cassandra's back, the one with the micro-millimeter bit. And I mounted it to the wall by the aquarium habitat and pushed the back of my head right into it. I had already drawn the eggs into a micropipette, which I inserted into the hole the drill had made. I pushed down the plunger and the eggs entered my head in the cool liquid of their solution.

At night when the lab was empty, I brought my daughter out of the cold room. I sat before the aquarium with her in my arms and I rocked her and even sang a little. The bees loved my singing, they grouped and moved in response, and their cousins in my head would stir, too.

"You must come home," Roland said to me during the days. "Come home and sleep in your own bed."

Fenn

But I stayed in the lab, took my daughter out of the cold and put her back, pressed my head to the aquarium glass. Lab corridors opened around me in pathways I could barely parse. Furniture, walls, windows, doors—a black-and-white flatness, a series of half-related outlines, a blurred environment of mere shapes. When the humans returned, I could smell their strange materials. Outside the lab the city stretched in a long, endless architecture of hard and erstwhile bewilderment. I stood and I saw a jumble of skyline and in the glass some odd features reflected —eyes that glittered above a slack and honeyed mouth that I could only guess might be mine.

When I opened the lid of the Los Angeles aquarium, the bees sensed it and pulsed, flew up and out, joined their relatives in the glass-fronted room, the Sierra habitat. I curled in my sleeping bag under flowers shaken by bees, gold bulbs of heat lamps, both colonies roiling above my aching, echoing head.

THEN CAME A SOUND—water moving, wind, the chime of voices. I opened my eyes to a network of trees overhead, a lattice of leaves and light that pierced the film of my eyes with its sharp points.

A figure shadowed the sky, brought a face close to mine, spoke some sounds, a mouthlike structure moving. "Tu es là," the mouth said, "l'endroit que tu aimes le plus."

One of the human languages. A name came—Jean—the name belonged to the face. I licked my lips, opened my mouth to respond.

"Wuksachi," he said.

Wuksachi, I began, but no sound came out.

"Je pensais que," he said, as the light pinwheeled down, sliced at my eyes. He switched to another language: "I thought, perhaps, it might help you. I brought you here to the mountains. The Sierras, your research station."

As I lay there, I could not help but pattern words, languages in my mind. Hallgrímskirkja, I said, the words high pitches in the air. Then: *Apis mellifera mellifera. Abeille noire.* (E)-9-Oxodec-2-enoic. Bee.

"What are you doing with your head. Your hands." He grasped at my fingers, which moved wildly in the air.

Guwahati, my hands said in his hands. Hypoxanthine. Athabasca oil sands. CCD.

His body on mine, a rucked root, beautiful and soft and hot, pressing down—pleasurable—on the bones of my chest, stomach, hips.

Mothers, I said against the skin of his back. Mothers. Mothers. I pulled him so close it might have hurt, but didn't. Some instinct came to mind then, our bodies locked in that ancient, mechanical dance—a joyful, muscular-skeletal coupling, needs dispatched, mutually advantageous, succinct.

But a sound was calling, a chorus, a symphony in the distance. I rose, left him in the grass, walked up the mountain toward the upper slope, the hemlock in the sparse grove.

Mud made an iron smell, clinging to my feet. The trickle of the snow-melt stream, clear water in it. I wanted to kneel, thrust

Fenn

the back of my head in the freeze of water, to quiet the buzzing, the heat, the ball-shaped swelling in the back of my skull.

But I didn't—I went on, I walked—I walked up the mountain, my head split with heat, shards of light, color, a field of shapes in which a ball of warmth pulsed in the tree at the top of the ridge.

Up the slope, up to the sound, the sound I could hear now as a chattering, a communication, a mass series of dispatches to my body, head, heart.

A hundred, a thousand bees, the swarm up ahead—their cacophony quickened, grew louder, a trillion miniature trumpets with stingers, excited at the sound—and sense—of my coming.

I came to the tree, wormholes in its surface, pulled at the wood. It came loose, the velvet thump of a soft skull-piece, onto the ground at my feet.

"Holy mother of God," came Jean's voice as he entered the clearing. "Holy of holies." The crack of twigs behind me as he sank to his knees.

There had been, in the composition of the hive, a drastic, spontaneous change.

Every individual bee in the hemlock was dancing in sequences reserved for queens.

When a hive realizes it has grown too large, it will send its queen out into the meadows. The queen will fly and half the hive will follow her, until she finds a new home for them all. From the eggs left behind, a new queen will be made—bees change their roles in response to the group's state.

The bees streamed from the tree, and they danced the queen's dance—the dance that tells the hive it's time to leave. The cloud swarmed around me and I was not afraid—I could see they could sense what I carried. In a boiling, smoky haze they swept fast up over the meadow, high toward the peak of the mountain. They gathered in a brooding, expectant woman-shape of queens, head trained toward me, expecting me to follow.

Jean muttered behind me, and I turned myself toward him, and I witnessed the horror on his upturned face. I could feel the change coming, a trickling through my ears, a trickling up through my eyes and throat.

Further up the mountain I knew a cave lay, and that cave is the place the bees marked for me. The cave lay behind a massive ice shelf where once I'd found a strange, unwelcome sight. I had come to this shelf in my early Sierra days, before I found the colony that was healthy. The ice shelf had stretched before me in a vast and pitted surface clouded all over with black dust. But the dust had not been dust—in fact it was bees, scattered there on the ice, in a sort of mass grave.

Behind the ice shelf, now, behind that frozen once-grave, my sticky form sutures fast and deep in a rock crevice. Outside the mother of queens, unable to reproduce, hovers in a swarm, a guardian attendant. I can feel my offspring coming, their strength and their newness, their resilience in the face of destruction. They'll have metallic bodies and the ghost of human thoughts and they'll walk across the land and be called daughters.

I do not know how many humans will remain, or if my daughters will view them with sympathy. It may be that with the changes I've made, my daughters will only feel sympathy for themselves. But I like to think, when I turn my thoughts to humans at all, that genetic interdependence might enable some mutuality between the species.

Fenn

I am here with an open mouth, a mouth full of royal jelly, and my daughters are creeping out from me. The mothers made their way to me with this riddle of feeling, to spin into the honeycomb of a story.

I don't remember now why I did what I did, though I know I must have had a reason. There was something in my body that I loved as I love my daughters, but I can't even remember what I was then.

MOTHER, GROW MY BABY

Sabrina Helen Li

(Winner of the Fall 2019 Aura Estrada Short Story Contest)

EDITOR'S NOTE:

Incantatory. Dream-like. Lyrical. Heady, like good red wine. A refreshing interpretation of the theme of allies. A poignant testament and exploration of "in-betweeness," of living in and negotiating worlds within and without. It reads like a condensed novel. Looking forward to more stories from Li.

—Yvonne Adhiambo Owuor, Fall 2019 Aura Estrada Contest judge

THE CHINESE WECHAT MOTHERS were the first to tell me I was pregnant. They know my body better than I do. I've known about the Chinese WeChat mothers since I was born but have never met a single one of them. My mother was added to the group when she went back to Shanghai to visit my grandma. Without even asking, my mother downloaded WeChat onto my phone. "They need to know you exist," she told me when she returned. "They will help you. They understand." I don't even know what the Chinese WeChat mothers look like. Their profile pictures are usually zoomed-in photos of their children's faces. The Chinese WeChat mothers never go by their own names, only by their children's, something like Meis_mother_828. The Chinese WeChat mothers are even hidden to themselves.

The Chinese WeChat mothers are there to make sure things go right. They exist to make sure mothering happens for little Chinese boys and girls the way mothering should—exact, methodical, constant. Legend has it that the Chinese WeChat mothers have always been a group, even before WeChat existed. Always waiting for a husband to come home, for a child to come back to them. Always looking forward to telling a new mother what can't be done.

The night they tell me I'm pregnant, I'm in bed with my husband. We've been married for two years. I lie and tell people we've only been married for a month. They bring up the fact that he's white less this way, certain the mistake will undo itself with time.

Every night before I go to sleep, I open up Snapchat and scroll until I get to the face swap filter. I only downloaded Snapchat for this filter. In the dead of night, I stretch out my right arm and hold my phone above our two heads. The phone screen lights up our faces and makes our skin look like shiny puddles of curdled milk. The first time it happened, I couldn't help but let out a tiny scream. Sometimes I get Max's eyes and he gets my nose. Other times, I get his thinner lips and he gets my thinner eyebrows. Each face swap is different—something newly stolen, newly returned. One time, the app didn't even recognize my face and only recognized his. I kept tapping the screen, willing the phone to see me. The phone always sees my husband.

The scariest though is when the app glitches and the image freezes. There's nothing I can do. I can't power off my phone or exit the app. I'm forced to stare at these sticky, horrid in-between versions of ourselves. I wonder if we're always just our own ghosts—our hauntings always being self-hauntings.

I've been doing the face swaps for years. I started when we were dating. At first, I did them to see what our children would look like, if they would be pretty hapa babies, if they would be Asian, if they would be white, if they would be mine, if they would be his. Soon, though, I began to think less about our future children. I wanted to know what parts of myself were the most resilient. I keep all of the face swaps in an album on my phone and scroll through them once in a while. The face swaps tell me more than regular photos do. I see what parts of myself I've allowed to be stolen from me.

My husband doesn't know about any of this. I only do the face swaps with him when he's asleep. Unlike me, he doesn't wake easily. My husband always needs sleep. He's in China every two months for the reality TV show he produces. When his work permits, he can sleep for thirty-six hours at a time. I've spent so much of our marriage alone with his body. I have no idea if he dreams and what he dreams about. I sometimes ask him when he wakes up, and he always says he doesn't remember. But in the end, he always comes home to me. He sometimes wraps me up until we're tight and pressed like a sausage. Right now, that's good enough for me.

The night the Chinese WeChat mothers reemerge, my phone freezes. Ever since I married Max, the Chinese WeChat mothers have texted me constantly. I quickly deleted the app. I even got a new phone and number. I wanted them to think they had lost me. That I couldn't be fixed.

Tonight, though, the app is back on my phone. Green, bright, and hopeful. I don't delete it this time. I am alone and the love of a thousand faceless mothers is better than no love at all. I stare at my phone, and my hands tremble as I wait. I throw my phone across the room and hope it breaks. Doing nothing was a mistake. You don't want the Chinese WeChat mothers to be in contact with you. It always means you've done something wrong. My phone begins to buzz violently with texts.

Stupid!

Stupid!

Stupid!

The texts flood over the frozen face swap until all I see is green. When my phone unfreezes, I open up WeChat and am not sure if I'm supposed to respond. I see three blinking dots bobbing up and down as they text me.

Why did you leave us? Why did you abandon us? Do you not love us?

I try to delete the app from my phone, but it won't let me.

Your mothers know. Your mothers know what you've done. You will regret this. You need to fix your mistake.

I want to scream, but nothing comes out.

There is a pause as the mothers type. Instead of text they send a voice memo. In a low, monotonous voice they cry out like a chant, *A baby knows the body it's growing in. Make sure it knows it's yours. We will help. Listen to your mothers. Your child is our child.*

I put down my phone and hold my stomach in my hands. I stare at my husband and think to myself *this would be the time for you to wake up,* but he doesn't. I look at my stomach, just the two of us. I wrap my arms around us and stay like that until morning.

ONCE UPON A TIME, my mother's greatest fear was that I would give birth to a watermelon baby.

When I was five, my mother left for three years to take care of my grandma in Shanghai. When my mother finally came home to us, she was obsessed with removing seeds, shiny and black, from fruits. The doctors said my grandma could choke on them, but my mother was certain it was something more than that. This was the first time she consulted the Chinese WeChat mothers. They said that seeds make the body haunted, make a woman shrivel up into herself from all that excess growing. Hunched over the kitchen table, my mother dug her nails into the wet flesh of papayas, dragon fruits, kiwis. She'd dig and dig until the black came out clean. She'd place each seed into a ceramic bowl and I'd stand on my toes and peer down. I always wondered how the darkness could look so full. Afterward, she would kiss my hair and make me touch her fingers, wrinkled and sunken. In a cracked whisper she'd say, "This is how much your mother loves you. This is how you will remain clean. This is how you will remain good." By myself, at the kitchen table, I'd eat the flesh she gave me, soft and browning, bite by bite.

My mother once tried to do this for my father, but he wouldn't listen. He wanted to eat food the way it was given to him, untouched by my mother. At night, my mother would take a pair of tweezers and remove the seeds from my father's fruit, doing her best to keep the flesh intact just the way he liked it. The next morning, the garbage can was overflowing with the fruit, shrunken and wet.

Li

Once when my mother was driving me to school, when it was the two of us and we were alone, she said, "Your father can eat like that but you can't. His body doesn't change in the ways ours do. His body is safe."

I nodded in the backseat and watched the black of my hair bob up and down in the rearview mirror like an insect trying to squirm to the surface.

"When I was gone, I hope your father wasn't feeding you food the way Americans sell them. Everything needs to be picked out. Everything needs to be clean and like itself."

"Yes, Momma."

"You know, Grace, you can't have more than one thing growing in you at once." I stared into the mirror and tried to find a version of my mother, but I couldn't see. "You'll never be able to get a good boy like that."

When I went to school that day, we had apples for snack time. I sucked on the seeds all throughout class, the little bits of black jiggling in my mouth. I caressed them with my tongue *one little apple baby, two little apple baby, three little apple baby, mommy loves you*. When a boy sitting next to me tapped me on my shoulder and asked what I was doing, I swallowed the seeds in surprise. I spent the entire recess in the girl's bathroom, forcing myself to throw up until three black dots landed in the toilet.

WHEN I DECIDE to tell Max I'm pregnant, my face is being pressed down hard into a mattress. Whenever we're about to get into an argument, Max will flip me belly first onto our bed and place his body on top of mine. We'll lie there, spine to stomach, and soon we'll start laughing. He'll start squirming on top of me and I'll start squirming back and we'll look like one dancing, decapitated centipede. These are the times I'm the happiest with Max. Our limbs moving on top of one another in sync. Whenever Max is on top of me, the mattress never groans. Some days he makes himself light for me, but today he wants me to feel his weight.

"Why are you on top of me? We're not going to fight."

"Really? It felt like we were about to."

"You always think that, Max."

"Why do I always think that?" My eyes are being forced closed by the mattress pressed against my face.

Max is white, but he's more Chinese than I will ever be. The show he produces is about recent widows who rent out actors to be their dead spouses. The viewers tend to hope that the fake couples will fall in love. There is always a live audience on set but they don't always participate. Their only job is to yell out "real!" or "fake!" whenever they feel like it. You never really know what exactly they are saying is real or fake—sometimes it's that the love is fake, sometimes it's that the people are fake, sometimes it's the words. Very rarely does the audience deem something real. My husband tells me though that it doesn't matter. That feature was Max's idea. He said it gets the audience at home to trust the show more. It scares some of the participants, though, who aren't used to being on TV. One time a widow was getting undressed after she thought the cameras had stopped rolling and from the faceless audience, someone yelled out "Fake! Fake! Fake!" With a scream, her body fell on the floor and coiled into itself like a snake. I wished her fake husband would have done something to help her even if he was just acting. Max used the footage as the trailer for the next episode.

Today Max just signed on to do season two of the show without telling me. The production company called the house and left a message for him. Max was supposed to be back in Boston after season one wrapped up. He's going to leave in a couple months, and live in China for a year. I just became a kindergarten teacher in Boston and can't move schools, especially to one in China.

That night, when we're about to go to sleep, Max says to me, "I'm sorry. I was going to tell you."

"Why didn't you?"

Max is silent for a while. "You never deal well with me leaving."

I tap Max on the shoulder and I can feel him move on top of me.

"Can we switch places?" Max always likes to point out how light I am. He jokes that I wouldn't be with him if he weren't so much stronger than I was. I usually don't mind it, but today I want to be heavy like he is. Today I feel powerful.

I slowly climb on top of his back.

"Am I heavy?"

"No. I could shake you off so easily, Grace."

"Let me be heavy."

"No." My husband laughs and starts to go up on his hands and knees. On his trembling body, I slowly rise. I press my body hard against his. I will myself to be large, massive, full.

"Max, I'm pregnant," I whisper in his ear. His body collapses and the mattress groans. I haven't even taken a test yet, but I just know. The Chinese WeChat mothers wouldn't lie to me. I stare at my husband and wonder why I didn't tell him sooner. I don't know what else to do so I start wriggling like a centipede—waiting for him to resume our dance—but my husband lies still.

IT'S TWO MONTHS into my pregnancy, and I only see my husband when he comes into our bedroom to give me food every night. He gives me bags of burgers and fries and chicken wings from McDonald's. Everything he knows I like. He even gets me a kid's meal ("for the baby, of course"). It comes with a little plastic toy. I roll the toy in my hand. The theme for this series is Parisian food—tiny baguettes, thin plasticky crepes that smell like chemicals, teacups the size of my nail. I hold onto them for the baby.

I've always wondered why children are so fascinated with fake food. We have boxes and boxes of fake food in my kindergarten classroom. Every so often, a child asks me why they can't eat the food that's in the play area, and I tell them that plastic children eat plastic food. But still, every week a child will swallow a slice of fake pear or a plastic square of chocolate or a glossy pat of butter. Why do we crave what can't be eaten? I sometimes wonder what would happen if we all just ate objects—notebooks, dollhouses, little toy cars—if that's how we became nourished. If instead of birthing people, we birthed boats and hats and stuffed animals. What would we crave

Li

then? How much simpler would things be? I hold my belly and feel the baby wrapped up inside me, swaddled in a brilliant ball of grease.

What are you trying to feed your baby into, nui nui?

I stare down at my stomach. I think of little plastic babies. I think of baby boats and baby cars. How nice would it be if the baby looked like nothing, looked like nobody. A blurry, buzzing, faceless head. A tiny plastic apple.

WHEN I WAS TEN, my mother abandoned me for the Chinese WeChat mothers. That was the year my father divorced her. That was the year that my mother became convinced that she was going to have a miscarriage. Two twin baby girls, both swallowing the other in the same gulp. That was the year she became convinced that I was pregnant. I had only gotten my period a year before. My mother was certain that her twin girls had fled her belly and escaped into mine. I held my ten-year-old stomach every night. I massaged the skin, tried to feel their heads, mold them into the shapes I thought they should be, and told myself that this is what it must mean to be a mother.

Every day for a month my mother would coo at my bony, thin-skinned belly. Every day my mother would go to the grocery store and come back home with crates and crates of seeded fruits just so that she could pick the seeds out for me one by one with her stubby nails. My mother waited in the shadows as I ate the fruit. She made sure I ate every single bite.

At the end of the month, though, when I still hadn't given birth, my mother began to get nervous. She took me out of school and told the principal that she had just had a complicated birth and needed me with her. She fed me constantly. Different fruits in different portions. Now I know: she was trying to build my baby for me. I remember that year drawing pictures of little stick-figure girls with fruit stuffed in their mouths, saliva and juice dribbling all the way to their barely-there nipples.

One night, I grabbed a handful of black seeds stuck to the side of the kitchen garbage can and went to my mother's bedroom. I shook her shoulders and swallowed the seeds one after the other. When I was done, I peered down at my mother through the darkness. She was still. Her eyes closed. I crawled back to my room on all fours, an animal, scared but full. My belly dragged on the carpet, and I felt my skin slowly begin to burn.

The morning after, I woke up to my shirt pulled up to my armpits, black seeds glued with spit to my stomach. I screamed, but my mother was gone.

After that, it didn't matter if I was pregnant or not anymore.

After that, my mother abandoned me for the Chinese WeChat mothers. She would drive off in our station wagon to an authentic Chinese restaurant forty minutes away. And she would come back smelling greasy and stale and bitter not at all like how my mother was supposed to be. She became a ghost in the house. I was only aware of her presence from the objects she moved—the glasses in the sink clouded by her lips, the warm chair jutting out at the kitchen table that I'd sit on and refuse to get out of until I couldn't tell if it was my heat or my mother's and it made me want to cry.

I always wondered if the WeChat mothers became her new daughters, if they became her new mothers, if they became her new husbands. Maybe their faceless bodies gracefully replaced us all.

MY HUSBAND ENDS UP going to China when I'm three months pregnant. He tried to get out of his contract but the show wouldn't let him. To make it up to me, Max sends me presents twice a week. Cheap silk slippers, plastic barrettes, pink qipaos in crinkly plastic bags. He gives me clothes that Chinese venders coax American tourists into buying. "You'll look so pretty in these, honey."

When my husband is gone, the Chinese WeChat mothers take the opportunity to convince me he is making my body haunted. They call my phone daily to tell me.

Can't you smell the haunting? The haunting has a smell. We can smell it from here. Your belly is rotting.

Nothing smells like itself. I want to tell them it's because I'm pregnant, but I don't. Whatever the mothers do, I always find myself picking up the phone. I always wonder when they'll call next. I don't want them disappointed in me.

While Max is away, the Chinese WeChat mothers tell me that everything Max owns is haunted. His socks, his briefcase, his razor. Even his side of the bed.

Cut the bed in half. Burn it. Keep your side. It's still good. Don't you worry, nui nui.

The Chinese WeChat mothers take care of me in their own way. They leave boxes of food by my doorstep every morning. Crates of curled-up chicken feet, white chicken smothered in egg whites, fatty pieces of duck drenched in hoisin sauce.

Guai nui, guai nui. Eat up. Fill yourself in the right way.

I eat every bit of food they give me.

WHEN I MISS my husband I like to watch his show. It only comes on at four in the morning, so I have to force myself to stay awake. On this episode, a widower is teaching an actress how to make a dish that his dead wife expertly cooked. It's chicken soup.

"Boil the chicken whole," the widower instructs.

"Can't we remove the head first? It's staring back at me."

"You're not trying very hard to be my wife then."

"Fake!" the audience yells. "Fake!"

"OK. Whole chicken it is."

"My wife always loved using all of the animal in our meals. Always making sure that we could taste it for what it really was."

"Real! Real!"

The next ten minutes consist of a time-lapse montage of the two cooking the dish, the widower hovering over the actress. At the end, the actress places the pot of soup in front of the widower, the chicken head bobbing up and down like a buoy inside the bowl. He takes a long slurp and the liquid dribbles down his chin like drops of piss.

"This tastes better than my wife's soup." The actress waits a beat to respond and glances out toward the audience.

"Real! Real!"

"Oh, I'm so glad," the actress says with a smile.

"Fake!" I yell out and turn off the TV.

I wonder if I died and if our baby died, if my husband could go on his own reality TV show. If he could get actors to play our dead selves. I wonder at what point the audience would yell out "Real! Real! Real!" to the actors. I wonder how long it would take for my husband to forget about us. I wonder how long it would take for me to become fake. Sometimes I wonder why he created this show in the first place, what exactly is in it for him.

I SPEND MORE AND MORE TIME at work as my second trimester starts. The house feels haunted. While I haven't thrown out my husband's belongings like the Chinese WeChat mothers have demanded, I have placed them all in a box and locked it in the corner of his closet. It's full of his belongings, but also the presents he's shipped to me. Boxes of key chains in the shapes of dumplings, fake jade bracelets that cost two dollars, shirts that read "Versachee" in big red letters. At first, I just avoided going near his closet, then the bedroom, then the entire second floor, now I'm afraid to be in the house.

Today in school I ask the class to draw a picture of their families. They create waxy stick figures looming over one another with big giraffe necks. They make their stick figures hold hands. They write out the names of their parents above their heads. I then ask them to draw their future families. "Now, what would my family look like?" The class pauses and some of the kids look at my stomach.

"Is that a trick question, Miss Grace?" a boy asks.

"No. I'm just curious."

"Shouldn't you be the one to draw it? We shouldn't be doing your work for you," the boy yells out.

The class watches as I go to the board and take out a piece of chalk. My hand shakes as I draw a large circle.

What will you draw, nui nui? We're curious too.

I draw myself. Long hair, small nose, thin neck.

"Hey, that's just you, Miss Grace. You cheated," the boy yells at the top of his lungs.

IT'S THREE MONTHS before my due date when I decide to surprise my husband by visiting him. I promised him a while ago I would see his work. This is the first and only time I'll be in China.

In China, my husband grows larger. Chinese women always ask to take photos with him. I'm the one who usually takes them. After the eighth group of women asks to take a photo, I whisper to my husband that we should start charging. He laughs. "Don't we need the extra money, Max?" His mouth straightens. "They're just joking, Grace. Let them have their fun." Max, like all men, enjoys being liked. Max, like all men, is able to say what is a joke and what is not—telling me if the things I believe are real were secretly fake all along.

Li

On the third day of our trip, my husband takes me to his work. I go onto the set and sit in the audience. The cast is in the middle of season two. Right now, a widow and an actor are performing the last conversation she had with her real, dead spouse.

They do one take of the scene, and the audience around me yells out "fake!"

They do another, and the audience yells out "fake!" again.

Through the blackness, I can see some of their faces, shadowed and smiling. They yell at the top of their lungs.

By the eighth take, I'm starting to yell "fake!" too. I feel myself smiling. There is something addictive in telling people what they are doing isn't real. That you don't believe them for a second.

It's the twelfth take now and from somewhere on the set, my husband yells out "Keep on going, guys!"

"Fake! Fake! Fake!" I yell at the top of my lungs. I feel my belly shake at the noise. As I continue to yell, I swear that I can feel my voice multiply, as if the Chinese WeChat mothers are echoing right after me. "Fake! Fake! Fake!" we all scream together.

IN THE END, I can't tell what race my child looks like when she's born. In a sagging bed at Mass General, I hold her at arm's length and look at her left to right, up and down.

"Put her back in! Put her back in!" I yell at the doctors. "She's not fully formed yet. I still need her in there. She isn't looking how she's supposed to."

The doctors stare at me and motion my husband to come over and do something. He comes over to my bed and rubs my back. He hands me a McDonald's bag, filled with the tiny plastic toys I had kept. I open the bag slowly. The baby immediately begins to claw at the bag and the toys fall onto her like fat, plastic raindrops. Before I can do anything, she takes a toy in her tiny hands and puts it in her mouth. In one swift motion, she swallows the plastic food and smiles. All of the doctors crowd over her at once. With thick latex fingers they try to open her mouth.

My husband takes the bag from me and clutches it at his side.

"What are you thinking? What have you done?" he whispers. My mouth feels wet. I'm scared to know what's inside of it.

The doctors aren't able to remove the plastic toy from my baby's stomach. They say they'll have to wait until morning when she's digested it more. I sleep with her that night, her belly on top of mine. I wake up every half hour to look at her. Sometimes she moves, and in response, I sink the small of my back as far into the hospital bed as it can go. My girl is young, but I want her to feel heavy. I want her to know that her weight means something. On the other side of the hospital room, my husband sleeps in a chair. I haven't looked at his body from this far away in a while. I stick out my thumb and move it to cover his body. He disappears in an instant.

In the dead of night, the Chinese WeChat mothers come to the hospital room. I wake up to my mother holding my baby next to me. Cooing at it, feeding it slippery slices of fruit. Beside my bed is a bowl of black seeds, and I place one underneath my tongue when I think she isn't looking.

My mother smiles at me. Standing in the doorframe are the Chinese WeChat mothers. In three gentle strides, my mother reclaims her position within the dark mass of the WeChat mothers. I can no longer see her. I sit up in bed to try to see their faces. The mothers move as one body. Shrouded in black, they slink to the corner of the room. This is the ultimate mother. This is where the shadows of all mothers go. I see one mother's face and it is blank, a blurring buzzing orb. They walk out of the room as one, my baby held in their many hands. The mother who I am almost certain is my real mother opens her mouth and all the other mothers are swallowed in one clean gulp. She looks at me as she leaves the room, and I fall asleep.

Real, real, real. She was very real after all.

ANOTHER WAY TO LOVE THIS WORLD
*Abdellah Taïa, translated from the French
by Amanda DeMarco*

WHEN I WAS LITTLE, my parents didn't do anything to keep the world, Morocco, and the men of our neighborhood from raping me. Raping me again and again.

It was an open secret. And a taboo at the same time.

He's a fag. He's a fag and he's for everyone. Help yourself. You can do anything to his little body with total impunity. Touch him. Caress him. Penetrate him. Hit him. Spit on him. Transform him into a sexual object for anyone who is sexually frustrated. He is a communal object. He doesn't complain. He's so docile. Such a feminine little thing, prancing around and getting everyone excited. Look, look how he walks and how he makes his eyes dance. It's his fault, let's go, let's go rape him. Everyone gets a turn. Everyone gets a turn.

No one will ever tell. It's like that here, and everywhere in the world. A universal law, I tell you.

Abdellah. That's me. They didn't call me Abdellah, no. For them, I was Leïla, or Zoubida. Or Sawssane. A boy-girl who wasn't supposed to exist and who, precisely because of this nonexistence, could satisfy their limitless libidos. A body on which a crime could be committed before thanking it with a smile. Yes, just a brief smile. That will be enough. He won't say anything. He doesn't need to. Everyone knows what he is. No one is going to go to the police. Nor the king. Nor the courts. This boy-girl is already protected. The devil protects him. He is the devil. He's not so innocent. Beware. Take another look at how he walks and how he talks. All of him is for screwing, for penetrating, from behind, his mouth, even his ears.

I still don't know how I survived. How I saved myself. And how I saved another as well, the little Abdellah I was. How would you have done it? Where would you have found the energy? The intelligence? What would you have told them to keep them from destroying you completely? But they did destroy me completely, what are you talking about! They tore me limb from limb. Very quickly I was no longer myself. I was evil. When they saw me pass, women said: there he is, there he is, that demon, that devil, he should change his name, Abdellah is a sacred name in Islam, he should change it and leave this place.

How old were you then?

I don't know, everything is mixed up, everything is jostled around. Ten years old. Twelve years old. Not more. I know that at some point, I thought that they were right. I was dead. And from that point, from that strange new place, I started to take more risks. To die a little more each day. Suicide, you mean? Maybe that was it, suicide, the idea of suicide, but that wasn't the word I had in my head. No. The word that obsessed me was revenge. What? You managed to get revenge? Yes, maybe. I'm not dead. I'm still here. That's your

Allies

victory, to still be alive? Really? Are you making fun of me? I did what I could at the time. Evil within evil. Evil further within evil. I stole. I lied. I prostituted myself. You prostituted yourself? No matter what you say, I am you and I myself don't remember that you prostituted yourself. You're making things up. No, stop contradicting me, I am telling you that I prostituted myself. Often. They gave me five dirhams, Henry's-brand cookies, ice creams, or brought me to the movies to see Bruce Lee and Jackie Chan. Fine, fine, I believe you.

Violence on the part of some. Silence from others. Rejection everywhere. And my heart, which isn't my heart.

But what must I have done to God to make him so angry at me that he punishes me like this, with the hard, agonizing members of these awful men inside me, deep inside of me? It's my fault, yes, I know, and it's up to me to get out of all of this. Alone. All alone. Forget God, he won't do anything to save me. Forget my father and mother, they're too poor and survival takes all their energy. Forget my sisters, life is even more difficult for them. Forget my brothers, they don't see me.

I am not a victim. I am not their victim. Despite it all, I'm not a victim, and if I become one then they succeeded after all.

I want my revenge. I cherish it within me, as a criminal project openly declared, justified, just, more just than their justice system.

I'm leaving this poor neighborhood, poor Morocco where the poor are forgotten by the rich, by the king, and are pushed to tear each other to pieces. I'm like them, I know it only too well. But to find the strength to go further into evil, I'll have to go to another neighborhood, in another territory. Far away.

Taïa

Where? Where did you go, little feminine thing, Abdellah? Toward prostitution again, is that it?

I went to look for strangers, to find in them the echo of what I am, the traces of my unhappiness and of my evil and of my blight. Strangers will see how dirty I am, dirty, defiled, defiled, defiled by everyone and by myself. Strangers who no longer believe in this world, in this heaven, and in this silent Allah, these blind parents, good beings broken before me, destroyed, pulverized and waiting for a miracle, the last light in the very depths of the dark well of this existence.

And did you find them?

Stop making fun of me! I know that you are me, but that doesn't give you the right to treat me like that, with arrogance, irony, disdain.

Go ahead, get on with your crucifixion. I already know the story anyway. You're going to tell us about the Frenchman on the beach of your city, Salé, is that it?

Yes. I have to talk about him. Yes. I have to talk about him. I believed that he was an angel. An ally. A sage. The Frenchman, white and pure. He was called Frédéric. He was handsome, Frédéric. Very handsome, Frédéric. He was on the beach of the city of Salé, yes. On the sea wall. At the very end of the sea wall. He wanted to watch the sun set. He was waiting. And not far from him were all of Morocco's rejects: drunks, the deranged, murderers, phantoms, sex workers, and sorcerers. Frédéric wasn't afraid to be there, surrounded by us, we who were so black and so dark and so bad. Maybe that was what attracted him, the beings at the bottom, on the ground, finished and, ultimately, free.

Free of what?

I didn't hesitate. I walked up to him and I sat beside him. I knew intuitively that he would love me, repair me, not do me wrong, understand everything, and, without a word, renew the energy and ardor within me, in my little body. Yes, you are going to do all of that, Frédéric. You don't seem like them, you're like us, these puny rejects on the sea wall of the beach at Salé. You're handsome and you're tall, you're like Jesus in the films I saw on television. The same whiteness, the same goodness, the same calm, the same beard, it makes me want to embrace you, to kiss your feet and hands and even dare to ask you for a miracle. You're beautiful, beautiful, beautiful, Frédéric, take anything you want. Of me. And everyone else. You're the Savior. I see you like that. You are the fresh blood that, mixed with my own, will shed new light on things. I will wander with you and on your body and in your skin. In that way, you will see everything and, in my stead, you'll say everything. I know that I ask too much, too much. I won't talk. You hear everything and you understand everything. A little effeminate thing, Abdellah, doesn't need to say the words, it's enough to look at her to grasp everything. And you understood everything, didn't you?

And he understood everything, this French Frédéric who was white like Jesus?

Yes. At first. The first time on the sea wall. And after that, the five other times, everything got dark, became tragic again. He was French and with that identity, he could allow himself everything. He could stop understanding us when he wanted. And help himself to what he wanted. Just help himself to us. To me. He did it as well, he made me lower my pants and his hard member spilled all his semen inside me many times. He never spoke. Never. Said nothing. Nothing. The man who said nothing and fixed things in me, in us, later became nothing more than silence that killed. That continues to kill. Like my father's silence, my mother's, the neighborhood's, Allah's.

Frédéric is a colonizer, that's all, Abdellah.

Stop boring me to death with your intelligent discourse. This word colonization, I didn't understand it, I didn't see it. I saw a white man who could go everywhere, and everywhere he could allow himself whatever he wanted. And he could leave. Leave without paying. That's what happened. He entered my ass ten times and he never paid. I should have made him pay, this Frenchman, stolen his money from him, his watch, his cross, started my project of revenge with him, treated him badly, badly, very badly, see what it was he hid so well under his white skin. Indifference and rejection, that's what he was.

What a romantic you are, Abdellah!

It's not my fault. It's not my fault. Egyptian films, the sentimental Egyptian comedies, ended up wrecking everything inside me as well.

And then?

Then . . . he left, Frédéric did. And two years later, he came back. In the same season. Same weather. Same place. The beach at Salé. The sea wall. The sun setting and growing red, blood red. I couldn't believe that he was there again, he wasn't ashamed, he said that he didn't remember me. Do you see? Two years had passed, I'd changed. You were changed then? I wanted to kill him, this Frédéric, to throw him off the other side of the sea wall, out where there were huge waves, waves that kill. He didn't have the right to come back here, to our place, the territory of the accursed, after what he'd done, leaving without saying goodbye, without even paying. But what nerve, how low! He allowed himself to go anywhere, this Frédéric. This is Morocco, it's not France anymore.

And you killed him, this Frédéric?

Yes.

Yes?

I spit on him. And I left again. I went to my neighborhood. The drama of departure, long after any hope was gone. Frédéric was hope. Then he was the death of hope. Even France, so seductive though I don't know why, could crush a little effeminate thing like me. In the mid-eighties, France had sent an ambassador, Frédéric, to transmit this message to me. I listened to him, Frédéric, speaking without speaking. I spit on him and I left again.

There's no more hope.

Love doesn't exist anymore. So, where to live? With whom? And all of this evil in me, in my heart, my blood, how to handle it, satisfy it? How to become someone else? How? Morocco and France seemed so allied against people like me. So powerful and so arrogant and so false.

The world is empty.

I am not a victim. I am not a victim. I am not a victim. Somewhere a pure source of life must exist. I have to find it.

And while you were waiting, what did you do after this French disappointment? Where did you find salvation and new allies?

I didn't find anything.

Taïa

I started to talk to myself. A voice in me spoke about me, in me, all the time. It said silly things. Grandiose phrases. But I let it talk. What else could I do? There was no more love, there was no more space for fags, then as now, it's the same tragedy and the same solitude. That they screw me, rape me, kill me. I want to die, to die now. There's no more love. It's certain from now on.

But you aren't dead, Abdellah.

I have to continue to love them despite everything. To cry, I don't know where, and to cling to them. After all, like them, I'm poor, a poor person so poor and so violated among the poorer of this Morocco so unjust to its own citizens. I have to love my father. I have to love my mother. They fed me, that's something. They let me sleep under their roof despite my reputation in the neighborhood, that's something. And my big brother, he's a hero. A hero lacking all sense and all courage, but I'm so in love with him, I want to be him, I continue to see him as a hero. My hero. The hero of the house. He's going to lift us out of poverty. He's a role model. He's culture. He's cinema. He's power. Our revenge. I'll steal everything from him. Make an ally of him in spite of himself. Suffer. Suffer, Abdellah. You are a disgrace, an obstacle in the path, the path of heroes, your big brother. Don't say anything. Not to him. Not to the others. Let them touch you. The cocks that enter you and spray their milk in you, you'll end up getting used to it. You're fifteen, that's already old. Don't be fragile, always sick, don't be a little capricious girl, take their cocks, take their semen. It's your fault, after all. And God really isn't happy with you. Do you understand? Love the world as it is. It is how it is.

I am not a saint. I need help. I'm not even a fixed identity. I'm nothing. I understand everything that happens in the world, I see it, I analyze it, but that doesn't help, it doesn't help at all. They've hurt me so badly.

Oh, quit moaning. You've caused hurt as well. Lots of hurt. Everyone suffers. Take your turn suffering. There's nothing new in this story. Suffer and one day, maybe, a hand will reach you.

A tender hand. A simple heart. A tender heart. A heart that holds the world. Somewhere it exists. In 1985. And in 2019. I know it. I know it. I can forget myself. I can. Hope that my ally is already walking toward me.

You're making a poet of us, is that it?

I was so small and they knew that I was homosexual well before I did. That's my misfortune. My truth will never belong to me. They knew about me long before I did, they knew everything my body said to the world without my permission. How to survive? How?

Listen to a song. Listen to Umm Kulthum. Listen to Samira Said and Abdel Halim Hafez. Listen to Ana Carolina and Caetano Veloso. Watch the films of your beloved Bette Davis. Especially *The Letter*, where she's a murderer and regrets nothing. Watch it again and again. Get out of yourself. Yes, get out of yourself. There's no more hope in you. Your parents aren't there anymore. They're dead. French Frédéric isn't there anymore. He disappeared. Your rapists aren't there anymore, they're married and have children now. But there are the others. The others. Forget yourself and go toward the others. Leave your little territory of identity, so safe, so certain, so petrified, which suffocates you a little more each day. You aren't just

Taïa

a fag. Look at the others. Take a good look. And hold out your hand. Yes, your hand. Your hand, your hand, please.

This hand, extended toward them despite everything, is your last hope. Do you understand?

Close your eyes. Open them. Get up. Walk. Over there, you see them, they're waiting for you. Go on. Go on.

There is another way to love this world.

AT THE GATES, MIKHAIL MAKES ME A FEAST OF RAIN AND DIRT

Hazem Fahmy

(a finalist for the Boston Review *Annual Poetry Contest)*

For which I'm truly grateful.
I've spent a lifetime dreaming
of cities wide enough

to hold me. I have feared open
roads; the seduction of
the unfathomable. All my life

I have prayed for a soil
unburdened by time, say an
Eden of a nap. And yet,

I sit before him alone.
He asks me about my kin
and country. I say: I am

sorry if I ever spoke
out of a mouth that was not
mine. I say 'we' and hope that means

something. I don't pretend
    to know where 'we' live. If there
is a place for 'us' I have

known it only by name, but
never map. I have looked for 'us'
  on the highway, only

    found sirens, restless screeching;
      choir of dust, shriveled lotus
    by an empty bank. Maybe

'we' are all just in love with
  scorched temples, dead languages.
Every dry river has a lake

    for a mother, and I am tired
   of the violence of water;
    how it holds the still land

with its ego. Somewhere,
  there's history without
burden. There is an 'us' I don't have

    to wash of blood and
     kerosene. Cut off my tongue
    if I claim I know what it

looks like, but hear me when
I say it does not smell
  like gated flowers, or stale fear

underneath a thick blanket.

I know I too am guilty

of this legacy. I have praised

the dirt I have spat on

only when it grows

what I ask of it. I've dug a grave

for every nightingale

who sang too loud. And for that you

can call my mouth rotten, but

never rested. الحمد لله

Insomnia's the only

vocab my city ever

gave me, and I speak it well,

let it overflow from my open

mouth unto the tired

earth. I know 'we' have all grown

weary from the taste of rust,

how its brittle trauma makes

a home out of our teeth. But

find me a history that

has ever undone 'us' and

I will go to bed tonight

unfazed by the summer. He

says: it is foolish to fear

Fahmy

the dark. I say: God gifts us
the night, and for that I am
eternally grateful. There

were days when I wished myself
small enough to die
in the flame of a lantern, but I

have settled for that music
which shakes the stillness. I have
mocked martyrdom's allure, I am

weak يا ربى I was
never near Bilal nor Omar.
Forgive me my timid jaw,

my quiet hands. They only
want to build.

Allies

THREE POEMS

C. X. Hua

(Winner of the 2019 Boston Review *Annual Poetry Contest)*

EDITOR'S NOTE:

*I kept returning to these poems. They don't beg for a reader. I could see no
way to extract one, to rearrange this sequence. I asked myself "Why these
poems?" the same way I might ask "Why do I prefer certain fingers on the
piano?" These have a light touch, flexible but precise.*

—Ladan Osman, 2019 *Boston Review* Annual Poetry Contest judge

Other People

My whisper goes to the piano bench,
the piano of bodies. Maybe what follows
is forgiveness, the error
of a fallen fingertip. You teach yourself to feel it
with repetition, like foreign language.
How to love this body.
How to love in this body.

Like touching, the work that's done
to tell time. On the other side
of the bed, what we'd call now, I felt a word
like *eléctrico, électrique, diàndòng* and rain. The death
of your mother entered our conversation with that idea
of the volta. So, I held your dead hand
and we bobbed behind her black hearse like ponies
in the old country, until each pulse dissolved into *pianissimo.*
The rest of that story is Italian, which I never learned,
all that time under lemon trees and parting. What dismembers
is only *la nube, as nuvens,* and memory like camellias
falling off their stems, like single hairs asking
how close one can get to the meaning
with exactly this much life to flatten
onto a page. My first ten thousand words
were Mandarin like ducks or oranges, were snow.
I say them slow as they grow forgotten, returned to noise,
molded and *wang le.* In the crystal vase, arranging
the spores and nouns of loss,
that infinite field of characters,
I feel the undersides of quiet growing.
I watch memories
spider into memories.
Turning towards you, again
I am listening for the one hot sound
to strike where the pain is most beautiful.

Nocturne

The shadow in the bed   wasn't your shadow.
Her hands still haunt you.
The record skips   on a rendition of Chopin
in the CD-ROM where 李云迪 makes
fast-moving romance   of mustangs and Polish rain.

What did your body sound like?

In another language, we were making fast copies
of such fresh pain it seemed
to be a copy of your voice—
instinctively, you hate how it sounds
maybe because it was yours yours
full of loneliness,
full of you.

Tulip fields wave repeat flags.

In a melodic arrangement of the timeline,
yesterday a man is asking me
why Chinese kids all seem
to play the piano   and I could only say
something like the sound a machine
makes when we call it music,
the string we brush and call a lifetime.

Hua

In the branches, a hooting tells me
about free will and terror.
This, I call regret.
We call it wood
when it's done with being a tree.

There are times this long search for beauty
feels like the breath passing through a harmonica.
You are trying to tell a piece of mahogany about
holding your skull in the bathroom mirror,
the nights it collapsed like a heartbeat.

You know vibrations through cold air will not save you.

Unthread the fog
and glimpse the mast going down.
Into the fairy tale, growing ever smaller,
she trades her voice for legs. Desire, how it leaves you
alone with the instrument of the body.

France

From France, I call my mother
to listen to her frail heart tell me. A thin stethoscope
branches, strangles through air, and the doctor's voicemails
say the mountaintops operate on subjective time. I journey
to the far left of a painting arrayed with lawn chairs, dappled
by a bath of sky. Lemon trees shade in
a slow poem about greenery
and promise. Briefly,
everything beautiful sits
outside the body. Every day, talking
on the phone beneath les orangeries,
studying the anguish deposited in each Rodin and cloud,
I consider the mistakes a pen makes out of landscapes,
our confrontation with Death in Romanic language
and the totality of raw stems for the dying:
Proto-Germanic and Saxon. Or Old English.
Parisian rain, umbra, constant theaters
for weeping. What I felt those days, I can only describe
in verbiage beyond my family's understanding,
another gallery of nothing. What was it
Barthes guessed about la mort, c'est
qu'il me faut perdre un langage.
In the sky's throat, the same
clockworks of mourning.
Every dusk, sitting silently

Hua

as available light gathered sadly
at the edges of that foreign country,
how we culled death or fate
as a tiny secret kept between us. Like a bud
or quark, unspoken and fundamental. Inside of time, how
there is no leafage too far away or broken.
At the end of a string, how you would say
anything to be heard.

TRANSLATION

Mattilda Bernstein Sycamore

(from The Freezer Door*)*

I'M PRETTY SURE there's nothing as sexual for me as walking shirtless in the hot sun toward the pounding bass of a sound system telling me I'm about to dance. The vocal in the song says "Just like 1994," which it's not, not at all, but maybe when I get home I'll look up this song that proves nostalgia now zooms in right to the time of my formation—the nostalgia of the early-'90s was all about the '70s, but now we have both and neither one is true, as nostalgia can never be, but anyway I'm dancing, that's the important part. I'm dancing outside in the blazing sun, shoes and socks and shirt off, sweat dripping down my face underneath the sunglasses and hat that are protecting my eyes from too much light. I'm dancing down at the bottom of the hill, right by the sound system, but only about four other people are dancing with me.

It's strange how rave culture might be the only place where I pass unintentionally—what I'm passing as I'm not sure but I guess someone who might have come here on purpose. And eventually there's some shirtless guy who looks like a fag, dancing with a blow-up toy and a lot of the guys here look like fags until you watch them interact, but this guy's moves are too overtly campy and sexual to be straight and then he's dancing with me, I think, I think he's dancing with me—and, yes, maybe I've passed the point where I should be dancing this hard, but the good thing about the grass is I can just fall, over and over and it doesn't hurt, roll around but now I'm jumping in the air, twirling around until he's the one who's tired I hold out my arms for a hug we hug goodbye it feels so good all that sweat like a real hug I want to see him again.

THERE'S NOTHING LIKE an election to make you feel hopeless about the possibility for political change. I pick up a magazine promising America's Essential Recipes, and open it right up to PORK SCHNITZEL. I'm laughing so hard that everyone at the co-op turns around to see if they can be part of my laughter. And then I'm walking through a field of dandelions. Even if it's really just the grass between the sidewalk and street I will take this field while I can get it.

The news is always its own trauma, but when the news of the trauma echoes into our lives, past and present at once, the open door never quite closes. Trauma as a curtain that billows around us, a wall we never quite break through. I mean trauma as a weapon. How to make oppression realize its redundancy. But oppression can never realize. Anything but oppression. How saying that something is structural means we need to take it apart or else it's a weapon we become.

How I can't go to a depoliticized vigil, I mean a vigil, which is always depoliticized, but walking past all the candles left out three days later makes me cry. How once we held political funerals instead of vigils. The power of grief in public spaces, but only if we're allowed grief on our own terms. How I can't listen to politicians telling me they're with me, and even worse is standing with people who are with these politicians. How assimilation even robs us of the tools we need in order to grieve.

Love is love isn't the most helpful rhetoric for those of us who grew up abused by the people who told us they loved us the most. They love us when we're dead, but they're not interested in taking care of us while we're alive.

I've never liked Robert Mapplethorpe's art, but I'm watching a documentary about him and suddenly I'm sobbing. Of course I knew the narrative ahead of time—but then: "You can tell how successful a show is by the sound in the room. On that night the room was silent." The night of Mapplethorpe's last show. He couldn't attend because he was too ill. Everyone peering into glass cases, and we're watching their watching. We don't know what they see—the recognition is ours.

How is it that recognition is always a shock? Recognition of self, recognition of feeling, recognition of impending death. Sometimes we think we don't need anything, and we need everything. And sometimes we know what we need, but we can't figure out how to need it.

This guy on the street says: How do you stay so blissed-out all the time? Which is one of the most confusing things anyone has ever asked me.

Sycamore

Confession: I just caught myself touching the leaves of a plant and thinking what is this made out of? One day, if everyone stops asking if I'm drunk, then maybe I'll drink again. How much is profound disconnection from humanity, and how much is utter loneliness? When I was sixteen, I went out to a club for the first time, and I heard Nancy Sinatra's "These Boots Are Made for Walkin'" mixed with some industrial song, and for years I thought that was part of the industrial song.

Sometimes they put a deceptively attractive exterior on a fake building, and suddenly it looks real. When people move in, will they look like this too? On the playground, this kid says: I need a translator, I need a translator to eat tonight.

I'm kind of entranced by watching these guys in the park touch one another so gently. Then I notice one of them is wearing an NYPD T-shirt and I want the world to end. Lying in the park trying to regain enough energy to walk home, I hear this guy circling around me, yelling in that language of conspiracy, internal made external, something about how if his people own this city how come he doesn't have shit and I know I should be thinking about the lack of mental health resources but instead I suddenly feel scared. Maybe because I drifted into something like sleep until the yelling woke me up. And I look at the other people in the park, one is staring at this guy and the other is still sunbathing—I'm getting ready to flee and I wonder if this is one of the reasons why we only have prison.

I'M WATCHING A VIDEO where two guys are talking about sugar apples for Christmas. In bed. In German. One of them is wearing a wedding ring—he's caressing his lover I mean husband and the camera is caressing his ring. I should turn this off now.

New scene. One guy has feminist theory on his floor, but the camera goes for his ass. In this scene the actors are speaking English. Everyone smokes everywhere—this is Berlin. I never realized I was sensitive to smoke until I lived in Berlin for a month, jetlag for two weeks and then bronchitis for the first time since I was a kid, and that was sixteen years ago but now even if I walk too close to people smoking outside it gives me a headache.

Everyone speaks English perfectly here—you don't really need German to survive, says this guy who doesn't speak English perfectly. But why are gay men obsessed with white sheets? Everything they could never have, a lifetime supply of Clorox to bleach out all the cum stains. Or maybe gay marriage keeps the sheets white.

I do like it when the guy with star tattoos on his arm says: Heterosexuality, what it that? Then he holds his cigarette to the other guy's ear as they start making out. I was straight in art school, he says, and they laugh. Okay, the making out is pretty cute.

But does this guy really have a huge cross tattooed on his back? Oh, they're laughing again—if only sex always included laughing, maybe we could live more for living. The guy with tattoos is telling the other guy he looks so much hotter in person, he should never bleach his hair blond again. The other guy says he likes it blond, it's going to be blond again.

But what's going on now? The guy who used to be blond notices scars all over the tattooed guy's arms—the tattooed guy is pointing out each of the places where he sliced himself—you do it this way, you do it that way. Cigarette burns—he's laughing.

It's so funny, isn't it, the other guy says. But it's like he's making fun of him, a challenge almost academic. Of course we underemphasize our wounds, those of us who must in order to survive. We laugh because this is what we know. I wish he would hold the guy with the scars, instead of challenging him to show emotion.

I keep rewinding this part that must be the key to why this movie matters, I mean suddenly matters for me. They're still talking about those scars. When was it, says the guy who used to be blond, and the tattooed guy takes a gulp of his beer and says: Reality.

What he would have said if they were speaking in German doesn't matter as much as what we know now. Trauma in translation. Translation of trauma. The reality of living. Living with reality. How do we make this possible.

SOMETIMES I WONDER if gated community is a redundant term. Creating boundaries around everyone who belongs, so that everyone who doesn't belong never will. I call Brian, and he surprises me by answering. Girl, where are you, she says, even though I'm calling from my landline. She's smashed. She says she's been thinking about me all day, she just wants to kiss my face—so then I'm getting ready to go to Pony, even though it's Pride.

I don't know if I've ever gone to a bar on Pride before. The best strategy is always to avoid as much as possible. But here it is. The moment I've been waiting for. Sure, Brian's smashed, but maybe this is an opening that will allow for a shift in our relationship. I need to take a shower first, even though Brian says come stinky. But stinky is not something I ever aspire to be.

Then I'm on the way there, and of course the whole street is blocked off in front of the Cuff, and the bass on the sound system is so loud that I kind of want to stay. Until the vocal comes on, and I realize they're playing "It's Raining Men."

The weird thing about being at Pony on the night of Pride is that everyone's so friendly. Usually people just stare at you and then look away, but now it's a constant stream of kisses and cruisy looks and Happy Pride, Happy Pride, so I figure I'll just smile and pretend that Pride can actually be happy.

Oh, there's Brian, in short-shorts and fuchsia lipstick, holding my hand and pulling me inside, where people are actually dancing, and then we're making out on the dance floor. And then in the photo booth. And then back on the dance floor. It's what I've been waiting for, but I can't tell if it's hot—I'm so used to desexualizing my friends.

Maybe I'm not totally present. Until we're back on the dance floor, now I'm dancing and it's that flirtatiousness with movement that gets me high, then we're making out and I push Brian up against the wall right when "Tainted Love" comes on—yes, really, "Tainted Love"—and honey, we are singing it. And this is when it really gets hot, my tongue going up behind Brian's teeth and I can tell he loves that, he loves all this tainted love.

Every now and then Brian says something like: I love your lips. Or: You're one of my favorite people. And: Is this OK? I hope this is OK.

You're giggling, Brian says, and he's right, I am giggling. I'm giggling because I'm in my body. I'm giggling because I'm having fun. I'm giggling because can't it always be this way. I'm giggling because we're like a performance, and it's also like no one else is even here. I'm giggling because Brian's spilling his beer all over my leg.

Someone wants to piss with us in the bathroom, but that will make me pee-shy so I piss in the sink. Brian gets another beer—I don't know how he's going to drink another beer. We're making out again, and he's rubbing my chest, yes, do that, yes, I like that, and I can't tell if he backs away because it's getting more sexual, and whether I want it to be more sexual now or to wait until later. I mean I want to wait until later, but also I want to feel this, so I know it's there.

I like how you can just be here, Brian says, and I know he means the way I'm interacting with everyone like I've been partying all day too—I just go right there, it's in me, it's in my history and anyway these people are more on my level when they're smashed, I mean in terms of a readiness for intimacy, a lack of borders, an openness to possibility. Yes, there's still shade, but tonight there's less of a gap between yearning and softness.

Brian and I go on the patio where we can't believe it's still so light out, how is it still this light? I guess it's just the difference between inside and outside, but still somehow it's surprising. Brian has to piss again, and I think of going with him to make sure he actually comes back, but then I think that's weird so I wait for him outside.

Someone's fixing her makeup, so I ask if I can look in her mirror to see if my lips or cheeks are covered in Brian's lipstick, and her friend says what are you looking for, everything is perfect. Bleached blond in a silver sequined dress like one of those women who's been in clubs for years I mean she's never left, I look in her eyes to see what drugs and we start dancing. The light is incredible, I say, and she says bring it down a little, I need something to cover this, and she points to her face, my eyes into her eyes and we're flying.

After a while it's clear that Brian isn't coming back, so I go to look for her, and there she is out front, all the way at the other end of the fence, making out with someone else. It's what I expected, but I didn't want to expect it so I decided to withhold expectation. It's not the fact that she's making out with someone else that bothers me, it's that she didn't come back to tell me about it first. I don't want to feel upset, but I feel upset. I don't want to walk back through all the smokers out there to get to her, and when I got to her what would I say?

I go back on the patio. Now I'm exhausted—what am I doing here? At least there's Amy, the woman in the silver dress. She says are you a Gemini—I knew you were a Gemini, I'm a Gemini, and there's that look in the eyes again, our eyes, and then there's John, who comes over and says you look amazing, what's your secret?

My secret is that I'm completely exhausted all the time. My secret is that I'm so absurdly healthy, but why doesn't it make me feel better? My secret is that I don't have any secrets. My secret is that's not really true. My secret is that I still haven't figured out how to exist with or without gay culture. My secret is that I'm so desperately lonely most of the time. My secret is that I do love it when people tell me I look great. I mean I'm trying. I'm really trying.

But now none of this matters because the music is so good, and I'm back on the dance floor. Someone impossibly hot taps me on the

Sycamore

chest, and says "You're breakfast," because that's the vocal—and she could be my breakfast, lunch, and dinner, but I don't want to do the same thing Brian is doing, I mean not until there's some communication between us, right, and now the communication is in my body throwing it down, flinging around, shrieking in that way that means there's nothing between my body and the world, this world of dancing and I know I should leave because now the smoke machine is on full blast, but I need to be here right now, with that dancing queen in the corner staring at me like damn, I mean she was doing that earlier too but then I went over to say hi and she couldn't speak.

Until I realize now, now's the time to go, while I'm feeling great again, before I crash, before it gets too late—I look for Brian again but I can't find him, so I figure I'll call when I get home. Amy's outside—she says I've been up for forty-eight hours, and you were just what I needed, I'm so glad we found each other. And then more kisses, more Happy Prides, and I'm out into the 10:30 p.m. but still not quite dark sky, where am I.

Back by the Cuff, there are so many discarded plastic cups in the middle of the street that it's almost like they were making a dance floor out of them. I'm thinking about how Pride is the one day of the year when fags can express their femininity and still be sexualized. And how depressing that is. So maybe it's strange to say this is the only positive aspect of Pride I've ever experienced.

And then there's that feeling that people are closer to the possibility of experiencing connection when they're smashed, and therefore further from the possibility of experiencing connection. This is what it means to celebrate. How desire and disgust can feel so closely related, surrounding self-actualization with self-hatred. Is this just true for queers, or for everyone? How a universal experience is universally impossible.

But I had fun, I'll admit it, I did—I'm thinking I need to look up that "You're breakfast" song. I'm thinking that I don't want to call Brian and act like I wasn't annoyed, but how will I do that? I'm so used to acting like I'm not annoyed, and how this shuts me down.

I get home, and I call Brian. Voicemail. I love voicemail. I can always say exactly what I want.

AGAINST TRAVEL: A COLLABORATION

Rachel Levitsky & Suzanne Goldenberg

Introduction / Rachel Levitsky

IN SPRING 2016, I taught a workshop for the Poetry Project called Prose, Prose! Many of the workshop participants were also visual artists. With one of the workshop participants, Suzanne Goldenberg, it turned out I shared a long history of early '90s NYC queer and radical street activism, although we didn't recall having ever met before. We kept in touch (as I did with many of the workshop participants), and the two of us met at my home in December 2017, where she modeled a drawing practice for me. I then offered her a methodology for writing prose poems that would be auto-editing, since editing/revising was a process that was proving to be continuously and profoundly anti-intuitive to her. Suzanne was on her way to Mexico, so I suggested that she write one daily and that each one be called "Against Travel." I had myself been wanting to write a book called *Against Travel*, so I decided to also follow the exercise/prompt.

For me the word "against" in the phrase is not merely oppositional; rather it evokes a general ambivalence about travel, the *against* of rubbing *up on* an object, a kind of disavowing frottage.

For over a year and a half, Suzanne and I have been writing these and sending a quick text of the poems as soon as we do. We collect our own and we don't speak to each other's content. It's a way of publishing ourselves to each other.

Here is the original exercise:

Each day write fourteen sentences in one sitting. They can be any kind of sentences, they don't have to be in paragraphs, they can be in verse or a list, or any combination and they can just be a block or whatever. No constraint there in terms of how the sentences sit on the page.

Each sitting shall include nods to or observations of:

—the weather

—a daily violence (don't ask me what this means)

—something that you did or made since the last sitting

—something specific to the place that you are (this could be the weather)

—something you remember that is past (this could be a daily violence)

At the end of writing it, type it if it's not already typed and send it to each other (or someone) in an email or text.

It seems important in a book about allies to mention that after the Prose, Prose! workshop ended, one of the participants, Carolyn Bush, a brilliant poet who cofounded the Brooklyn arts nonprofit Wendy's Subway, was killed violently by her roommate. She was twenty-five. Wendy's Subway

Levitsky & Goldenberg

now has a book award in her honor. Then in July 2019, another participant, Em Samolewicz—who had continued writing and painting, and who taught art to children and yoga to people of every body type—was killed in Sunset Park while commuting on her bicycle. Em was thirty. She was the eighteenth cyclist killed in New York City this year. The community of poets is close and exists as much in honoring and remembering the lives and work of those who've passed as it does in celebrating and publishing those who remain. I want the work of the beloveds I have lost to continue existing in literary, social, and political space. I feel that their work wants this too.

Against Travel / Rachel Levitsky

For Suzanne

I call them books. Every attempt to tell the story foretold as yet to be. I was of the strong opinion it should be long. Is long that what's sliced by an aftermath of something tragic. That heads injured by the very blow are held on repeat swinging around to look again. Is each of these an exploration of form? I say I'm writing about language. I want to look the way people look who get lots of sex but get fucked with less. Aging means more dye. I returned to the book of poems in which the lesbian playwright's lesbian sister asks a lot of vapid questions that the evidences show are read as meaningful to many. Prizes. Am I stupid or guilty or on a different page? That's the question I was looking for but instead got the one that says, yup, I have no idea what will happen next, just that I wait for it looking with eyes backside my head. To be alive is to wait like this, an anxious proposition. We know it might be very bad. Chances are. And love she who resists naming the question, who when asked loses the answer.

tu casa / Suzanne Goldenberg
from Mexico: Against Travel series

cortez kicked them off the mountain so they moved
some say simple words still like holy shit and give me some fuckin oral sex
now you're singing in your sleep &
playing music too early
drown out the cock's crow stain inside drawing is still the best way. to
go or eat with friends
to cook is to be alive eating even better blasting harmonica is not what
i hoped
so early on new years day but its what you love
and i'm a guest here
i hug who u hug and dance when u dance
there's less competition when it's all in the family
i was just happy for a quiet moment but now its gone
a headache takes over takes its place
not a clean window for miles
and you went way too far to come all this way to listen to bad rap before
ten am
it's (not) the end of the world

CHAPATI RECIPE

Noel Cheruto

(a finalist for the Aura Estrada Short Story Contest)

1. IN A LARGE BOWL, stir two cups of flour, one cup warm water, salt and sugar to taste. Add a spoonful of oil. Knead to a thick consistency. Knead slowly, feel the elasticity of the dough pull at your shoulders, down your spine, to your thighs. Your pale thighs spotted with blue-black patches of hurt. Wonder how it is that he hit you only in hidden places: above your knees, around your belly, under your armpits. Know, as you know night from day, that he spent all day every day thinking up new ways to torture you.

    Show them to your friend, over breakfast: your skin in different shades of broken, your hair falling in sad chunks off your dry scalp, your numb heart. Hike your skirt up in the middle of her kitchen, with one foot up on a chair, the other on the cold tiled floor. Tell a story to go with each scar. The dark blue one near your crotch is for when he couldn't find his tie, the brown one that looks like a tiger stripe is from the day his soup was too hot. The yellow one that looks like a hand hugging your breast . . .

Watch her hold her teacup to her lips. Freshly brewed ginger tea, you can tell from the scent which lingers at the back of your throat. Watch her cradle it with both her hands, absently blowing at it. Her nails are little neat red squares. Watch the steam blow off the rim and up her nose. Her nose is sharp and bent into the brim, like a hook. Watch her pull up a noisy slurp, stiffen her back and ask, "You can leave him if you want, but who will provide for the child in your belly?"

2. COVER THE BOWL with a clean cloth and allow the dough to rise for an hour. Wash your sticky hands in the sink, pulling away chunky bits and letting them flow down the drain. Wave through the window at him, sitting under the tree on the lawn. See him smile, bare his even teeth with the tip of his tongue showing through, like his father. His legs are spread out, with the left bent at the knee. His hands hold a yellow book between them, index finger hovering impatiently at the top right edge of the page, ready to turn. Exactly like his father. Your son, your little savior, all grown and tall. Wonder whether he too will wake his wife with a stiff punch to the gut one night because she was snoring. Blow him a kiss and soap your hands.

Your son, the first time he kicked in your belly, you forgave. You gathered all hurt, wrapped it in a bow, and set it aside. No funeral, no vigil, nothing. Just one moment filled with pain, the next a kick that stretched your belly from the inside, and right after, peace.

You were outside your friend's house when it happened. The morning after your husband led his Air Force colleagues in a failed attempt to overthrow the government. You waited patiently for her pity, knowing she was afraid but hoping love would triumph over fear. She did not come in the morning when you wailed outside her gate like a beggar and told her they took your husband; she did not show her face at noon when you sat out there on the curb shielding your face against the sun with your purse. She did not come in the evening when the sun began to set, sinking your hopes with it.

He chose that moment to announce himself for the first time, your son. Three kicks that felt like he was trying to force his way out of you. Right then, with the last light casting long shadows across the tarmac, you realized that no one was coming to save you. You gathered your belongings—your big brown purse, three banana peels turned black and limp, and one large scarf around your waist—and walked away.

3. PINCH OFF fist-sized balls and roll these into flat circles. Circles you turned in the morning of the coup. The day the Kenya Air Force took over President Moi's government and then lost it back in under an hour. You sat on the purple armchair in the corner of your bedroom and listened to the radio. You turned your back away from the window and waited for the sound of his car.

Hear it now, as you did then: the soft voice of a radio announcer being cut short. Know, from the sound of him, how he looked at that moment, announcing that they had taken over the government. Know it because you had put little flags of warning around his moods as if they were a minefield. A low, even-pitched voice with slurs at the end of each sentence meant medium risk. If, however, the voice was accompanied by rippling muscles up and down his arms and a tight jaw, best to brace for impact. Know, then, on that day in the radio station that his shirt sleeves were folded up to his elbow, his hands wandering to the back of his neck and rubbing vigorously, his eyes steady and unblinking.

You looked everywhere for him after the coup. Looked without hoping to find: in the morgues, overflowing with dead bodies, in hospitals, prisons. Everyone—people you knew and those you didn't—flooded Uhuru Park the next day to pledge allegiance to the president. After that, life went right back to rolling along. The shops on River Road continued dispensing Omo washing powder and Cowboy cooking fat, the tailors along Kenyatta Avenue went back to laughing and sewing, the parking boys around Odeon Cinema picked back up their glue tins and sniffed as if nothing had happened. Nobody came to help you.

Nobody looked you in the eye—not friends, not strangers. Even in his absence, he found a way to punish you.

President Moi, deeply shaken, changed that day. He went from a compassionate leader to a paranoiac who rewarded only acts of loyalty. Corruption went from taboo to norm in the feeding frenzy that followed. Laugh at how he inadvertently accelerated the very thing he was trying to prevent.

4. HEAT OIL in a shallow pan and fry each chapati until golden, like the sun on the day you met, in the arboretum. The sky was cloudless. Little purple flowers that looked like whimsical bells in a child's drawing fell off the jacaranda trees onto the grass.

Cheruto

There was a small stream behind a clump of bushes whose trickle sounded like a soft clap. The day was hot and windless.

You were at the same friend's birthday party. She had everyone put on white T-shirts with her name printed across the back in black. Everyone had on blue jeans. You played a game where you all stood in a circle and threw footballs at each other. He threw his at you every time. You failed to catch each one.

He came to you later, standing over you so that your legs were under his shadow. You ate sliced pineapple, picking up the slices with a fork and holding them away from you, letting the juice drip through your fingers, down to the grass. He ate oatmeal cookies, stuffing large pieces into his mouth and chewing impatiently.

He talked about Karl Marx, and you nodded and thought about how lean he was. His long arms bulged gently in his shirt. He spoke of Che Guevara, and you made sounds of agreement and thought how smooth his voice was. If you had a voice that beautiful, you thought, you would be president or a radio announcer. "All this," he said, sweeping his arms outward in the general direction of the trees and the sky, "is not ours to divide and own. We are only to keep it safe for the next generation." You agreed and thought about how exceptionally brilliant and handsome your children would be.

He lowered his voice so that you had to lean in to hear him as he said: "Your T-shirt is too tight. Let us get you a larger one."

Feel in your stomach what you failed to acknowledge that first day: a desperate need to make happy a man who chose unhappiness.

ACTIVATION INSTRUCTIONS // UNTITLED 3D POEM
Amy Sara Carroll

Cut along the dotted lines.

Remove the poem from the book and the page.

Fold along the solid lines.

Experiment with alternating the poem's interior and exterior.

Affix tape to the box that the poem's become to concretize one of its configurations.

Fill the poem-box with other poems, paperclips, coquinas, raindrops, particulate matter.

Pass the box on to a stranger, to the love of your life, to your sworn enemy, to the person you know and don't know each morning metro platform.

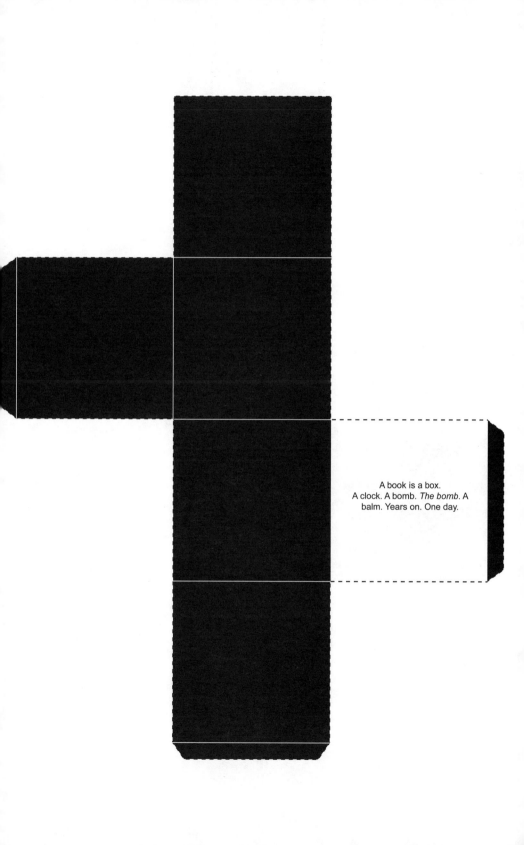

A book is a box.
A clock. A bomb. *The bomb*. A
balm. Years on. One day.

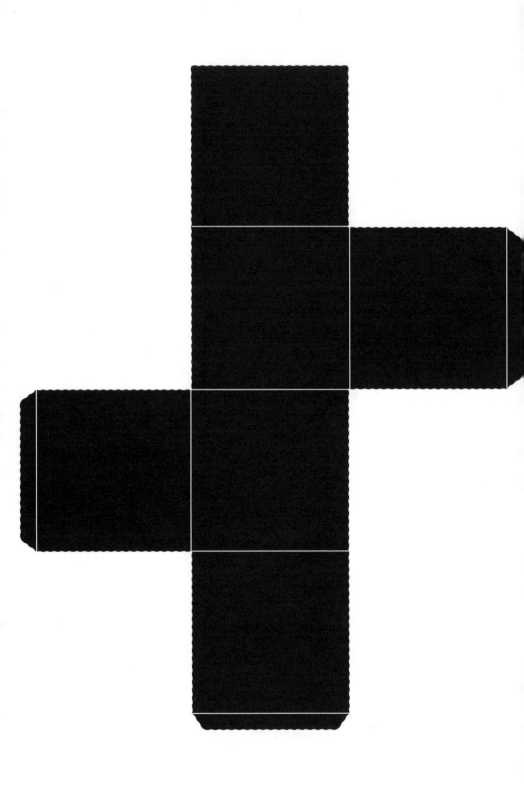

A BRIEF HISTORY OF THE SOCIAL JUSTICE ALLY

Micki McElya

AT THE START of 2019, gay journalist Jonathan Rauch proposed that the term "LGBTQ" be retired as a collective referent for sexual and gender minorities. To replace it, he recommended a single "Q." Writing in the *Atlantic*, Rauch argued that the "alphabet soup . . . has become a synecdoche for the excesses of identity politics—excesses that have helped empower the likes of Donald Trump." Careful to note that he was not drawing a direct causal line from the term "LGBTQ" to the Trump presidency, Rauch nevertheless claimed that it was just this sort of "balkanization" that fueled the resentment of "ordinary Americans" and alienated "white, straight, male America," sending them fleeing into Trump's embrace. While Rauch noted that the "Q" would be derived from "queer," itself an increasingly common term of inclusion in popular discourse, it would be sheared of the word's ugly history and more recent "radical baggage." His solution would make clear "that discrimination against sexual minorities—or for that matter sexual majorities—is not the American way."

This tossed-off aside about sexual *majorities* is actually at the heart of Rauch's argument about what is wrong with LGBTQ: unlike the longer initialism, even white, straight, male Americans can find a place for themselves in "Q"—or, more to the point, not feel excluded from it. Rauch is far from the first to think that a principal failing of LGBTQ is its lack of space for others. Indeed, this is a critique that has long been internalized: in the most common extended version of the term, LGBTQIAA+ (Lesbian, Gay, Bisexual, Transgender, Queer, Intersex, Asexual, Allies, Plus), a space has already been made for "Allies," who could be any straight person—even white, male, American ones.

The concept of "allies" is old, bringing to mind everything from World War II or the machinations of legislative bodies to the plots of most procedural dramas, but the current political meaning of the term has no real connection to these prior usages. Quite the contrary, the idea of the ally as someone who is not like you and does not suffer the same oppressions, but who supports your struggle for rights and freedom, is of recent vintage: it originates in the multicultural education initiatives of the early 1980s. How then did the idea of the ally become central to gay and lesbian activism and recognition, and through that to the work of present-day coalition building, from mainstream left politics to Black Lives Matter?

IN THE 1980s, higher education in the United States followed a corporate human resource trend: augmenting equity and compliance measures with new focus on the development (and administration) of diverse organizations and institutional cultures. In universities, this proliferated as a host of diversity programs, aimed at students as well as employees, which were interconnected with efforts to diversify course content and pedagogy. Focused on representational diversity—different faces and backgrounds among student populations, faculty, and university administrators—rather than the underlying structures and inequities that were the sources of underrepresentation, these programs tended to shift the burden of creating diverse institutions from the institutions themselves to individuals: if the university was not diverse, it was not because of administrative choices, but the failures of community members and applicants. The migration of such programs from corporations to universities not only constitutes a key site for tracing the corporatization of higher education, but also marks the ascendancy of the neoliberal university, with its defining free market logics and relentless promotion of individual choice.

This rise of diversity programming was in some senses a backlash to the civil rights movement and the cultural nationalism of Black Power, the Chicano movement, and others. Writing in 1989, feminist scholar Chandra Talpade Mohanty described university diversity initiatives as an emergent "Race Industry." They came about, she argued, in response to the radical pluralism of 1960s and '70s activisms and early implementations of affirmative action and education reform. In practice, they were "responsible for the management, commodification, and domestication of race on American campuses." A central feature of this management, Mohanty noted, was its production of a "harmonious empty pluralism" drawing false equivalents across various categories of difference, obscuring variability within those categories, and abstracting each from their history and structural specificity—the hallmarks of mainstream multiculturalism. The result was the appearance that significant diversity had already been achieved and more was on its way, while no meaningful institutional changes or redistribution of authority and resources had occurred. This version of diversity was not only incapable of addressing the compound conditions of structural inequality, but reinforced them by celebrating the existence of the diversity initiatives themselves. In the thinking of university leaders, if these programs failed to produce more diverse institutions, it was not because of their obvious inadequacies; it was instead because of personal failures—not least of all the failures of minority individuals for lacking the merit, character, or grit to succeed.

By naming this the work of a "Race Industry," Mohanty pointed to the fact that late-century multiculturism took its legal architecture from the longer histories of U.S. attempts to remedy racial injustice, from Reconstruction and the Fourteenth Amendment through the Civil Rights Act. By adopting race as the controlling metaphor for all kinds of injustice, multiculturalism sought to coopt the moral power and human bravery of the still-recent civil rights movement—particularly a version that privileged individualized over collective solutions. This was best represented in the period's common plea, based on the heavily redacted words of Martin Luther King, Jr., to simply judge each person by the "contents of their character." By the same stroke, it provided the emergent "ally" with a usable past found in Atticus Finch and the bloodied white faces of SNCC activists.

McElya

Coming from this world of institutionalized multicultural and diversity programming, the first printed use of the term "ally" in its present sense is in *Beyond Tolerance: Gays, Lesbians, and Bisexuals on Campus*, a 1991 resource manual published by the American College Personnel Association. The book's penultimate chapter, by Jamie Washington and Nancy J. Evans (one of the books coeditors), is called "Becoming an Ally." Evans also wrote the manual's introduction, in which she explains the need for such a book, the first of its kind, to her audience of other U.S. higher education counseling and student affairs professionals: "Although discrimination and prejudice related to racial and ethnic background are beginning to be addressed on campuses, oppression based on sexual orientation is frequently a taboo subject." The implied race-then-LGB formulation assumes racism as discrimination's ur-form, while also suggesting a bureaucratic structure in which non-white and LGB people are administered as distinct constituencies for programming and care. The verbiage also implies that these categories are mutually exclusive, reinforcing the presumptive whiteness of lesbian, gay, and bisexual people and their allies.

Beyond Tolerance posits the self-actualizing "heterosexual ally" as analogous in development and values to the white advocate for anti-racism. Washington and Evans take their readers through a comparison to a five-stage model of white identity development in relation to understanding racism and white privilege. The fifth stage is "Action," which they describe as the "most important" and by far the "most frightening" for straight allies-in-the-making because they must confront and overcome the "many challenges and liabilities for heterosexuals" that discourage most from public LGB advocacy.

For Washington and Evans, one of the greatest risks to the LGB ally is that people will assume the ally is lesbian, gay, or bisexual. This is an issue with no obvious analogue in anti-racism: it was rarely the case that white civil rights supporters were accused of being secretly black. Yet it has long been a stereotype that anyone drawn to LGBT activism must themselves actually be LGBT, and either unwilling to come out or still struggling to figure it out. For this reason, Washington and Evans suppose that only the most self-aware, secure heterosexuals can become allies. But the benefits of their bravery are many, assure the authors, including: the possibility of interacting with "an additional 10% of the world"; feeling less constrained by dominant sex and gender roles; having "close and loving relationships with same-sex friends"; possibly being the reason a family member, friend, or acquaintance feels secure in their LGB identity and doesn't turn to drugs or alcohol; making a difference to youth; and having the chance to be "invited to some of the most fun parties, have some of the best foods, play some of the best sports, have some of the best intellectual discussions, and experience some of the best music in the world, because everyone knows that lesbian and gay people are good at all of these things." The authors identify the last one as a joke—except not: "Imagine what it could be like to have had such close friends as Tennessee Williams, Cole Porter, Bessie Smith, Walt Whitman, Gertrude Stein, Alice Walker, James Baldwin, or Virginia Woolf. Imagine the world without their contributions."

Nearly everything on Evans and Williams's list directly, even exclusively, benefits the ally: it is unclear how, if at all, they advance the political cause of an oppressed minority. In spite of this, Evans and Williams insist that straight allies are critical to changing campus cultures, creating environments in which LGB people are safe and can thrive, and strengthening wider movements for equality. Straight allies may be most effective at raising the consciousness or changing the minds of other straight people, they contend, thus producing more allies. But it remains the case that the benefits they promote in order to achieve these outcomes are narrowly framed as self-improvement, greater self-esteem, pleasure (including the pleasure of moral righteousness), and the implied opportunity to moonlight as oppressed while knowing that one can always retreat to the safety of privilege.

UNTIL ALLIES WERE INCLUDED as equals within the LGBTQ+ cosmos, it had never been the case—and certainly not in the civil rights movement—that allies were afforded equal footing as an identity group within a social justice movement. There is, indeed, something deeply unsettling—and simply *incorrect*—about counting straight allies as potential recipients of harm and discrimination on par with lesbians, gays, bisexuals, transfolk, and other dissident sexualities and genders.

That said, it is impossible to separate the publication of *Beyond Tolerance*—and the early-'90s push for campus LGB initiatives and support services—from the HIV/AIDS crisis and its attendant safe sex education. Recall that in Tony Kushner's *Angels in America*, which premiered in San Francisco in May 1991, the central redemptive arc is of the unlikely straight ally Hannah Pitt, a devout Mormon who is mother to a closeted, self-loathing son. In the course of the play, Hannah cares for, and then becomes close friends with, the prophet Prior Walter, a gay man living with AIDS. In the end, the role of the ally liberates Hannah, opening her to a kind of self-knowledge denied to her son. This is to say, the ally was part of the Zeitgeist, and for many people suffering with AIDS, allies could mean the difference between life and death—or, at least, between dignity and dying alone.

Nonetheless, there remains an unsettling dissonance to the incorporation of an explicitly heterosexual identity category into a grouping of sexual minorities. For one thing, it is predicated upon the ally remaining demonstrably and steadfastly impervious to any fluidity of desire or gender expression, which seems both un-realistic and an unfair price of admission. More concerningly, the role of the ally as created by 1980s multiculturalism offered white heterosexuals a *minority* identity—as compensation for feelings of exclusion, accusation, and guilt—in a way that prefigured the rise of white-as-oppressed-minority identity politics in the age of Trump. This version of the ally was (and to a large extent remains) a liberal mirror image of the white backlash and ethnic heritage movements of the 1970s that gave energy to the Silent Majority and made the Republican Southern Strategy such a long-term success. While the New Right was animated by charges of reverse racism and special rights for minorities, the ally would come to represent positive white, straight, and/or male identities untarnished by structural privilege and relieved of complicity and negative self-image.

Although standing as liberal counterpoint, the ally simultaneously represented the wholesale incorporation of the terms of New Right challenges to pluralism and distributive justice though the insistent glorification of individual character, merit, and, to borrow a twenty-first-century keyword, resilience. In rejecting their own privilege and standing for or with the reviled, allies assumed sometimes-great personal risks to support the freedom struggles of others. They, too, became heroic, systemically harmed individuals who overcame their circumstances and could be celebrated for their moral characters, conviction, and selfless actions.

As multicultural pedagogies gave way to social justice education initiatives in the twenty-first century, the distinct silos commonly inhabited by white allies, straight allies, and male allies were dismantled with the embrace of intersectionality. In time, Evans and Williams's straight ally became simply the *social justice ally*, a more flexible identification representing the intersecting identities, oppressions, and conditions of possibility experienced by allies and the diverse communities with whom they align. It is in this version, for example, that the ally shows up in current struggles for racial justice. As many leaders of these movements have already noted, however, this configuration is no less troublesome, and for many of the same reasons: at its worst, the social justice ally is paternalistic and patronizing or playacting, putting on the suffering of another for pleasure, then taking it off whenever privilege suits them better.

Perhaps the notion of the ally will prove most productive in acts of its rejection, such as recent calls from activists for *accomplices* in social justice work, rather than *allies*. Recent research on ally development, particularly in the areas of higher education administration and social psychology, show a marked shift in their approaches, focusing on the ally's limitations and framing alternative models for affinity and teaching humility.

While inevitably freighted with the history of its origins, the ally remains to me a fundamentally optimistic and potentially radical notion. It carries the promise, if not always the practice, of relational politics and meaningful community; of new world making. I conclude, therefore, with both hope and skepticism. The historical record brims with unexamined privilege, brutal self-interest, lost opportunities, and the adaptive tenacity of neoliberalism. But it is hope that fuels change, that gave rise to the very idea of social justice education, and that sustains the spirits and labors of diversity officers and student affairs professionals who believe that "another university is possible" in spaces lovingly carved from oppressive institutions. It is the hope for radical transformation through the supple activisms of diverse coalitions forged in collective rage and mutual compassion. It is the hope of looking for—and looking to be—an ally.

THE PRIVILEGE OF THE ALLY

Rigoberto González

I FINALLY SAID IT aloud on a panel at AWP (the annual creative writing conference organized by the Association of Writers & Writing Programs). I don't remember which city, but I can't forget the gasp from a fellow panelist, a Native American woman who immediately wanted to rein in my "hostile language." Meanwhile, the poet sitting next to me, a Palestinian American, gave me a discreet thumbs-up. The entire panel—on addressing whiteness—was made up of poets of color representing various ethnic groups. The presumption was that we would unite our experiences and observations into a collective wisdom.

But the presentations became more and more tense as we took turns to address one of the moderator's questions about forging alliances with other groups. It made the assumption that all ethnic groups belonged to a single coalition. I cringed, as if we were supposed to break into song celebrating diversity and solidarity. There were barely audible groans of protest and disagreement on the stage, but we got through the conversation without bloodshed. When it was time for the audience Q&A, however, I unleashed what many had been thinking: that we have to privilege the mission of activism over bonds with outsiders because people of color tend to prioritize healing others' wounds before their own. This self-harming altruism has, in the long run, distracted from important work at hand and exhausted us.

That pivot played out like this: a young African American woman stood up to tell us that her women's group, mostly black women, welcomed white allies, who had over the years helped advance the group's projects. Yet there was this new member, a white woman, who was too vocal at times and assumed the position of power when the group had to make important decisions. When this imposition was addressed or even named, the woman would burst into tears, feeling offended and underappreciated. "What should we do?" the young woman asked our panel in earnest.

I chimed in immediately: "You might have to ask her to leave the group."

After my copanelist's disapproving gasp, I elaborated and informed the young woman that tactics like these were not the work of a true ally but of a narcissist intent on replacing any issue on the table with her own emotional needs. "Your group has to ask itself," I said, "whether it wants to expend its energy in comforting her or protecting the health of all the other members."

Perhaps the fact that the young woman nodded her head tipped the scales of tolerance from my fellow panelist (and a few members of the audience who glared at me from their seats). I had presented what struck some as a radical solution, but I felt the young woman had likely already considered it. She simply needed affirmation from someone outside who understood what her group was enduring. It wasn't about getting rid of the weakest link; it was about cutting loose the dead weight.

At the end of the panel, as people scurried to their next event, the young woman stayed behind to thank me—and to apologize for any negative energy directed my way as a result of my answer. "No need to apologize," I said. "And despite this response, I still believe these panelists are my allies. I can accept disagreement and even pushback. But I will never accept a relationship in which I'm forced to work on the feelings of a single person over my own or my organization's goals."

The young woman leaned in to give me a hug and then we both went about our business. The next hour of panels was about to begin.

I should clarify that I don't go around looking to exclude people. Such decisions should be left to the collective. It's important to understand how an organization benefits from outsiders and how it might be slowed down by someone—even an insider—who takes up all the air in the room. I learned this from my mother, an undocumented immigrant who worked in a packinghouse for many years.

For the Mexican women in the Coachella Valley of Southern California, an alternative to the backbreaking work in the agricultural fields was backbreaking work in the packinghouses, where harvested dates, corn, and carrots were sorted, boxed, and shipped out to the rest of the country. The hours were long and made longer still when a truck needed to complete a full cargo. The women were expected to remain at work, sometimes past dinner. I remember those evenings when the men had to round up all of us children and we shared pizza and liters of soda because our fathers were too tired to cook or didn't know how.

Workers would complain but only to each other. If anyone dared approach the supervisor, she was simply told not to come back. "Go to the fields," he threatened. "See how much easier it is there." At least, that's how my mother reported it.

The pay was low and there was no overtime. So when the United Farm Workers Union got involved, everyone knew that a strike was likely if negotiations were to fail. This was an ambivalent solution; the undocumented workers, including my mother, feared that the supervisor would simply call the border patrol and have them deported, thereby stomping on the fire of the protest and, more insidiously, breaking up the families of this community. When negotiations did fail, it was time to weigh the positives and the negatives and then put the matter to a vote: to strike or not to strike?

A labor union organizer was making the rounds to discuss this with one group at a time. Since most of the women in the neighborhood worked in the packinghouse, they gathered at the local church that gave mass in Spanish. All of us kids had to tag along. For us it was just another excuse to visit with each other as we squirmed on the uncomfortable wooden folding chairs. I didn't pay attention to most of the proceedings, but when my mother stood up, I perked up my ears. My mother, usually reserved, gathered the courage to speak out against another member, Carmen, who was not thinking through the options with the others but trying to convince them not to strike, jumping to her feet and arguing bitterly whenever anyone else spoke.

Carmen also happened to be our neighbor, so there was plenty of risk for my mother in doing what many other women couldn't accomplish: convince Carmen that this was a cause worth fighting for, or at least make her listen for a change. The labor organizer looked exasperated but she was too polite to tell her to calm down. Frustrated as everyone else, my mother quieted the entire room when she addressed the gathering: "Now let's all decide whether or not we will continue arguing with Carmen."

Shocked, our neighbor protested immediately. "I have as much of a right to speak as you or anyone else in this room, Avelina. I'm not going to be silenced."

"But you have been silencing everyone else," my mother said. "You refuse to listen and you've made your position known repeatedly. Unless that position changes, there's nothing more to your words except noise that's wearing us out. We need to make a big decision about all our futures, but you're forcing us to make one about you and only you."

The rebuke stung the neighbor, who finally relented and sat down. During and even after the strike, she refused to talk to my mother. But this only proved that my mother had been correct about Carmen, who was turning a group decision into a personal one.

I take my mother's insight to heart whenever I consider accepting support or advice from any person outside *or* even inside of my immediate circle: Are they going to help or hinder?

As a Mexican American, I have been heartened in recent months to see Catholic, Muslim, and Jewish activist groups, in particular, organize and protest immigration policies: the bans, deportations, detentions, and the dreadful caging of minors, children of undocumented border-crossers. These disparate groups may not have been working in conjunction, but their energies and a common adversary have the effect of a dynamic and multivalent movement, empowering others across the spectrum of identities and faiths into action and awareness. Never Again Action—chanting in Yiddish and getting arrested for disrupting ICE activities and speaking out about the United States' twenty-first-century concentration camps—is one of the clearest and most poignant examples of what makes a true ally: commitment to the greater good.

Allies, after all, can't hold a movement or organization back, not for any notable period of time. But they can fortify a mission, a goal, and the resolve of a crusade. We become stronger with allies, but we don't become weaker without them. Let's not forgot: the ally has a privilege that those in the fight may not have—simply to walk away, no harm done to the self, but maybe leaving some damage behind. I hold allies accountable or I let them go, if that's necessary to redirecting the focus back to more pressing tasks. The struggles continue, regardless.

SAY SOMETHING

Tananarive Due

JOHANSSEN WAS THE WHITEST PARK in the whitest neighborhood in the whitest town where Caitlin was living her whitest life, a shiny bubble of curated playground equipment and soft rubber chips in case of unexpected falls. No urgency from the outside world would ever drown out the giggles of toddlers clinging to swings, or the shouts from older children jostling skinned elbows on the basketball court. Caitlin hadn't planned to live in a mostly white neighborhood—especially in Southern California, of all places—but here she was. In her mostly Cuban American high school in Miami, *she'd* been the minority and rolled with it by getting an A in AP Spanish. In grad school, she'd come close to marrying Debashish, but she'd steered clear of the family drama (in fairness, mostly from his father in Kolkata) and married Tad from IT at the boutique publishing house where she edited art books.

Tad was the whitest name imaginable. When she tested Tad early on by praising Black Lives Matter, he'd said, "I understand what it's like to stand out—I have red hair," but she'd forgiven him and restrained herself from tweeting it out with a GIF of a head banging on a desk. God help her, maybe that drop of ginger exoticism *had* been one of the reasons she'd agreed to go to dinner and a Dodgers game with Tad and then ended up at the altar beside him two years later. That, and he was one of the few straight cis men she'd met in her dating life who wasn't a transphobe and homophobe, and their shared passion for the environment and horror movies sealed it. Their daughter, Destiny, had inherited his bright red hair, and it was true Destiny got teased, mostly for the freckles spraying her nose.

But still.

Here she was, a German-Irish white woman stranded on an island of whiteness, and she had *chosen* this; she had chosen to live in a place that did not feel like the country where she had grown up. How hadn't that mattered more when they bought their house? Sometimes Caitlin went days without seeing a black person (*African American*, she had been told by Latrice, her freshman roommate at UCLA, was a term used mostly by white people who did not have black friends). Sometimes she backed out of her driveway on Monday mornings without even noticing the silver-haired Latinx woman who had been cutting her grass for three years.

She didn't wear the political T-shirts in her bottom drawer, even her '08 Obama shirt, because her reputation as "fiery," as an ex had once called her, only went so far. She was not "fiery" at Johannsen Park. She spent too much time fighting with trolls on Twitter, so when she took Destiny to the park, she did not want to know who had voted for whom, or who thought "Fake News" was a real thing, or accidentally land in a dueling T-shirt contest with Mr. Blue Lives Matter, who pushed his daughter beside hers on the swing.

But two black boys were at the park now. A whiff of hope at last.

The boys—one about eight, and one, his brother, she assumed, about seventeen or maybe younger, but tall—had just started coming to Johanssen two or three times a week, probably from the new apartment building near the railroad tracks. Caitlin fixed a ready smile whenever one of them passed, to the point where last week the older boy (Shaun, or DuShaun) had given her a mistrusting glance. Which was fair. Too much, maybe. She had offered the younger boy (Trey, Ray, or Dre) a juice box when he was standing at the periphery of Destiny's birthday party this past weekend, but he had politely declined. Stranger Danger. Good for him.

The older brother was mostly babysitting; he walked his brother to the fenced skate park enclosure and said "You good?" and then went on to the basketball court with a ball pinned under his arm. He shot baskets while he waited; he missed some, but he hit most of them. Pickup games came and went around him, but no one invited him to play and he didn't look interested in joining. He checked in on his younger brother every fifteen or twenty minutes, then an hour after they arrived, sometimes more, he told his brother to stop flying in the air and they walked toward home, the younger boy riding his bright red scooter around him in zigzags.

Caitlin sometimes noticed flashes of the younger brother's skin in the skate park's blur of motion. When she heard crying after a fall, she glanced to be sure it wasn't him, since no black mother ever joined the row of parents waiting for wails or tears on the benches observing the playground and the skate park. These boys' parents probably had to work. It was a luxury, Caitlin reminded herself, to be sitting at a park at three o'clock on a weekday afternoon.

Caitlin was the only mother at the park who noticed the police car.

She spotted the black-and-white pattern slowing beside the basketball court where the older boy, Shaun, was listlessly shooting baskets alone at a hoop a universe away from the group of white teenagers at the other end of the court. He was so far across the court that he was closer to the street than the rest of the park, flanked by tightly packed houses. A white man stood in his yard with his hands on his hips, watching the court. Watching Shaun.

A drab day snapped to Technicolor.

Caitlin sat straight up on the bench. She turned to an invisible person beside her, as if to touch her on the arm, some shared recognition, but she was alone. On the bench across from hers, a young couple with a fussy toddler did not see the police car. Same for the retired woman who always did tai chi under the oak tree, her thin limbs flowing with colorful batiks.

Police drove past the park's basketball court often—*too* often, Caitlin had decided—but they rarely parked except when teenagers congregated at the curb, sometimes vaping. A kid had revved up his motorcycle too loudly and gotten sharp words from a passing officer during Destiny's birthday party, but that was as exciting as the park got.

Caitlin had never seen the police car door open, or a uniformed cop step out.

A *white* cop, she couldn't help noticing.

Shaun, if that was his name, was so absorbed in shooting baskets that he didn't seem to hear the snap of the cop's car door closing despite the echo in the cracks between the neighbors' houses. He stayed poised for his shot, measuring the distance. His basketball sailed and hit the rim, bouncing rogue. When he turned to chase his ball, he saw the cop coming toward him and stopped. His ball rolled to the sidewalk.

The cop, who was shorter, already had his hand poised over his gun.

"What?" Caitlin whispered. She stood up, fumbling in her back pocket for her cell phone.

The afternoon looked like a police video she had already seen, except in color instead of grainy and gray. The other teenagers stopped their game to stare where they stood, watching.

"I need to walk over there and see what's going on," Caitlin said to herself, and was disappointed when she realized she was not, in fact, walking over there. But she did manage to will her trembling fingers to find her phone's camera app, and then she was staring at the image on the screen of her feet standing still on the gum-stained sidewalk.

She was too far away to shoot video. She would have to move closer.

Yet, she wasn't moving. Her breathing quickened as she stared at their interaction from a helpless distance. The cop and Shaun were talking back and forth, so she filled in the blanks:

—*What's wrong, officer?*

—*Can I ask what you're doing here?*

—Shooting baskets. Clearly.

—Can I see some ID?

—I'm a kid, so I don't really have ID.

—OK, well, watch yourself for existing out here in Whiteytown.

Caitlin prayed the officer would walk back to his car and Shaun would retrieve his basketball, unbothered, but it didn't seem to be playing out that way. Shaun was frustrated, arms outstretched, and the officer's hand was still close to his gun.

The officer made a sudden motion with his hand, and Caitlin was sure she was about to watch this child get shot—adrenaline showered her in a way she had only experienced her senior year in high school, when she almost drowned at the beach. But the cop brought out gleaming handcuffs instead. Caitlin read Shaun's body language from a distance: *What for? What did I do?*

Caitlin had already taken her first steps toward the basketball court before she remembered to glance back at Destiny, who was taking turns sailing down the slide with her friend from kindergarten, Katie, whose mom was reading her Kindle on a bench on the other side of the playground. Caitlin waved to Katie's mom (Cynthia? Sarah?). Nothing. She waved again, and Katie's mom looked up from her reading. Caitlin gestured she was stepping away. Katie's mom nodded and put her Kindle down, vigilant.

Mothers looked out for each other's children at the park. That was the custom.

On the basketball court, Shaun's arms were posed behind his head. The cop was doing all of the talking now. Caitlin glanced at the skate park and hoped to see little Ray, or Dre, oblivious and happy on his scooter. But Ray was standing at the skate park entrance staring wide-eyed toward the basketball court. "Isn't that your brother?" she heard a girl behind him say.

Ray made a start as if to run, and Caitlin spoke to him more sharply than she'd intended. "*No*," she said, and he froze. "You stay here. I'll check it out."

Because not only had the police murdered Tamir Rice while he was playing at the park, they'd arrested his distraught sister too. Caitlin doubted that anyone else at Johanssen Park had heard of Tamir in Cleveland, dead for five years. But she had.

"Wonder what he did," Caitlin heard the tai chi lady mutter behind her.

Little Dre, or Ray, made a decision, dropping his scooter on its side. He took running steps toward the basketball court.

"Ray!" she called, and he turned mid-stride, confused. She'd probably called him by the wrong name. "Take my hand. I'll go with you. Don't go by yourself."

Stranger Danger forgotten, the child slipped his sweaty palm into hers, his heartbeat thrumming through his skin. He might be closer to six than eight. Closer to Destiny's age. Caitlin's heart was pounding too, but she hoped he couldn't feel it.

"What's your name?" she said as they fast-walked to the basketball court's asphalt past the huddle of watching teenagers. The smell of their sharp perspiration stung her nose.

"Trey." She almost couldn't hear him, his voice was so soft.

"What's your brother's name, Trey?"

Trey didn't answer, perhaps suspecting that he had misplaced his trust in this wild-eyed white woman who was interrogating him like the police. But he did not let go of her hand.

The cop had pulled Shaun's hands behind his back, snapping the handcuffs in place. Shaun was two inches taller than the cop, and she wondered if maybe he *had* done something and she just hadn't seen it. Was he a neighborhood drug dealer like in all the shows on TV? Was Trey an Amber Alert abducted by his older brother? Caitlin felt foolish, her face flushing with hot blood. Only her promise kept her walking.

A few feet away, she could hear Shaun, deep-voiced and angry on the surface but whining with childish fright underneath: " . . . that's B.S. Just tell me *why*." A second police car pulled up behind the first. The lights flashed, spraying red across the houses.

Trey was crying as he walked beside Caitlin, but she didn't have time to soothe him.

"Nice attitude," the cop said to Trey's brother. "Just keep talking."

Before she remembered to slow down so she wouldn't startle him, the cop looked up and saw her. He was young, maybe not even twenty-five, with a Marine-style buzz of light brown hair. He looked from Trey back up to her, puzzling over them. His face was soft until he saw the cell phone in her other hand. She didn't raise it to record his face. Not yet.

"Step back," he said the way he might have in Kabul, as if her phone were a weapon. The cop from the second car was moving in fast to back him up, hand also near his gun. He was Asian, at least, which was a relief, but what if most cops were blue first?

"That's my brother!" Shaun said, objecting more to Caitlin than the police. He must think she was a social worker.

Caitlin released Trey's hand and took a step away from him like a hostage negotiation was underway. And wasn't it? This might be the most foolish thing she had ever done, rushing so close to this scared armed man and a scared teenager this way. More foolish than wading to that sand bar so close to high tide when she was a high school senior. With so many guns, this already felt like drowning.

"Trey asked me to see what's going on here, officer," Caitlin said, trying to match the cop's authority despite her pounding heart and the way the basketball hoop seemed to wheel overhead. "Can you please tell me that? What's going on—exactly?"

The Asian cop waited, watching. He didn't know what was going on either. In a dreadful moment's silence, she wondered if any of them knew.

"We got a call from a neighbor," the first cop said. He didn't gesture, but when Caitlin looked at the shirtless man staring from his sun-browned little yard across the street, he moved to the protective shadow of his porch. He was afraid of her phone too.

"A call about what?" Caitlin heard herself say. "He's just playing basketball. He comes here with his brother all the time."

"You know him?" the Asian cop said.

"Yes," Caitlin said, and it was true enough to her. She knew enough. "He's just a kid. Why are you putting a kid in handcuffs? This feels like profiling. Isn't that what this is called?"

Caitlin had expected to approach with *yes, sir* and *no, sir,* but she had never been so angry at a stranger. With a trembling hand, she realized her phone *wasn't* recording, not even sound. She must have forgotten to press the record button, and the screen had gone black.

But the cop didn't know that. She raised her camera as if she were taping.

"Calm down," the first cop said, although he sounded uncertain now.

"You need to take these off me," Shaun said. "I *told* you. Profiling."

The cops shared a glance and communicated in silence. Then the first cop unlocked the handcuffs. Trey shook his hands as if they dripped with acid.

"A neighbor reported a suspicious person, and he gave me attitude," the first cop said. He was explaining his side to her, trying to shift the blame to Shaun as if he should not be apologizing to him instead.

A lecture blistered behind Caitlin's tongue on how anyone would be upset at being harassed by a cop and handcuffed for no reason, but instead she said, "I can tell you for a fact that he wasn't doing anything wrong," Caitlin said. "A *fact*."

The cop shrugged. "You know what they say: 'See something, say something.'"

"Yes. Exactly." For the sake of peace, she didn't say more.

The cop pursed his lips, annoyed. He glanced at her prop phone and decided to let it go, motioning to his colleague. They went back to their cars without looking back. The neighbor across the street slipped back into his house.

Trey ran to his brother and slipped into his arms like he was wrapping himself in the branches of a tall and mighty tree.

"I'm sorry that happened," Caitlin said. "Do you mind if I ask your name?"

"Ron."

Wrong again. And he was tall, but his face had baby fat. Maybe he was only fifteen.

"Are you okay, Ron?"

Ron nodded, rubbing his violated wrist. He seemed dazed, avoiding her eyes.

"If you ever have any problems here, you can look for me," she said. "I'm Caitlin."

He nodded again. "Thanks," he said. "Thanks for that. I was like, what?" He seemed to consider telling her more, but the memory already made his shoulders droop.

"I wanna go home," Trey said, muffled by the folds of his brother's jersey.

Ron's voice grew tender. "Where's your scooter? Let's go get it." He was eager to move away from a stranger's eyes, away from the moment.

As the two brothers walked back toward the skate park, the basketball sang against the concrete as the boys who had not been handcuffed resumed their raucous game. Under the old oak tree, tai chi lady was lost in her slow dance.

"Mommy, look!" Destiny called from the top of the slide, waving to Caitlin before she launched herself down its spiral, her red hair flying behind her.

Caitlin never saw Trey or Ron at Johanssen Park again.

THE HISTORIAN AND THE REVOLUTIONARY
Walter Johnson & Tef Poe
interviewed by Mordecai Lyon

WALTER JOHNSON, a historian at Harvard University, has written for
Boston Review about the role that guns and race played during his
upbringing in Columbia, Missouri. With books such as *River of Dark
Dreams* (2013), he has made a reputation as one of the most astute
chroniclers of American slavery in the academy. His upcoming book,
The Broken Heart of America, traces the history of U.S. imperialism and
anti-blackness specifically through the history of St. Louis. Climbing
the stone stairs to the Victorian he shares with his family, I notice
the front door is wide open. Inside there is a comforting chaos: toys
across the floor, stacks of books, basketballs, newspapers, shoes of
every size, style, and color. I am unsure whether to knock or call out.

Johnson is hosting our mutual friend Tef Poe, one of the central
organizers of the 2014 Ferguson Uprising. Poe is a St. Louis rapper
and revolutionary devoted to dismantling white supremacy and
shedding light on the city's history of black greatness. Poe and I met
at the end of 2018, when he visited a class I was auditing at Harvard

called The Historical Philosophy of W. E. B. Du Bois. The course was taught by Cornel West, who has mentored both Poe and me for the last several years. After traveling together to Puerto Rico and St. Louis, Poe invited me to help him with his forthcoming memoir, *Rebel to America*.

To those who know only one of the pair—a middle-aged Harvard professor and a millennial revolutionary from the North Side of St. Louis—it might come as a surprise that Poe is godfather to Johnson's youngest son. But the two have a strong bond of both personal and professional admiration, forged through their shared commitment to fighting anti-blackness and white supremacy. Since 2017 they have been working together toward the goal of creating a community-based arts center on the North Side of St. Louis (a story in and of itself). This fall they are cosponsoring a fellowship to support photographers and other visual artists from St. Louis, culminating in an exhibition that will travel between St. Louis and Harvard.

In this interview, they share some of the history of their friendship, their shared activism, and the place they see for allies—accomplices, even—in the long struggle for racial justice.

—Mordecai Lyon

MORDECAI LYON: Walt, how did you first meet Tef? What sparked your interest in his work?

WALTER JOHNSON: I had been working on the political economy of Ferguson. I looked online and found a video of a city council meeting in which Tef was just taking these people apart. He was lucid and on point and unforgiving, implacable. He was just speaking truth to the city council.

I thought, "Who is this guy?" So I read some of the stuff he had published in St. Louis's *Riverfront Times*. I remember one piece in particular, "Ten Disturbingly Racist Things About St. Louis," which was both hilarious and insightful, but was also stretching the category of racism—trying to speak to anti-Asian racism and Islamophobia, for example.

So I invited Tef to give a talk at Harvard, and it was fantastic, with about a hundred people in the audience. Tef brought a lot of energy and a lot of insight. He said that he had already become really engaged in the question of Palestine and of trying to build out from Ferguson. He cited Bassem Masri, but he also explained that the Ferguson protestors had learned how to deal with tear gas from Palestinian women who were in the protest.

That was interesting to me because it illustrated how everyday contacts or solidarities get built out into a larger sort of solidarities and political critique—how people start from where they are and move out. That's something that I heard Tef talk about over and over again. He would say, "Well, I have developed a large-scale theoretical opposition to homophobia because there were gay men and women on the line with me in Ferguson." To build out from that kind of immediate solidarity to larger sorts of political commitments. I thought that was really inspiring.

Johnson, Poe, & Lyon

He came into Harvard generous and open and wanting to teach, but willing to answer questions that probably struck him as hopelessly naïve.

TEF POE: I think the reason I can come into spaces like that and not take out my own pretensions on the rest of the room is because if I did, I would be walking around mad all the time. Like: seriously. I did do that at a point, and I was pissed off *all the time*. I don't try to embrace people as if what I'm seeing tells me anything seriously about you.

I come from North St. Louis, the damn slums of the slums. Places where, you know, they might as well have bombs dropped on them. So, to come out of that and interact with the rest of society, I had to learn how to make no judgments based off of what I see. I can't come in and hack off what is human about you. My interactions are about who the actual person is.

WJ: I'm a professor and I've written about social movements, and been involved in a few things, but, compared to someone like Tef, I don't know a whole lot about how actually to build a social movement like they built in Ferguson. The agonies, the personal stress, or what it actually feels like to be under fire. The extraordinary solidarities (and animosities) that come out of that kind of frontline experience. All those things are things I didn't know about then and really don't know about to this day, even after writing a book about St. Louis.

There's a version of the relationship between Tef and me that could be narrated as, "Out of our friendship, Tef came to Harvard." There's a comforting familiarity to that story because that's how we're taught power flows, but for me the real story is that Tef introduced me to St Louis. Tef helped me understand the city and the uprising. Tef put me in touch with Percy Green, who was a hero of the 1960s and '70s movement. Tef put me in touch with Jamala Rogers, who was a leader in St. Louis and nationally in the '80s and '90s, and directs the Organization for Black Struggle, an organization with which I've since been able to collaborate on a few things.

Tef got famous for many things—*Cheer for the Villain* should be the thing he's most famous for—but one thing he got famous for is saying, "This is not your daddy's civil rights movement." A lot of people took that as a dig against prior generations, but I don't see it that way. I see it as a critique of a set of middle-class concerns around a narrow notion of civil rights. To see how respectful Tef is of movement elders in St. Louis, how much he is willing to learn from them and invoke them—that stands as an example for me of Tef's generous attitude toward people in general. He's just a very nice person. But it also helps me think about the history of St. Louis, how it is that these folks are connected to one another. Tef knows Jamala Rogers, Jamala's married to Percy Green, Green was part of demonstrations against the racist hiring practices of Jefferson Bank in 1963, where he walked alongside black communist leader Herschel Walker from the 1930s and '40s. Green invoked the general strike of 1877 when he was trying to get a general strike going in 1979.

ML: We tend to think of the front line only as going up against cops, but the front line is also where people like us are having these conversations, are sharing ideas and resources.

TP: That's one of the reasons why I could rock with Walt. Even if he didn't understand it at the time, that's what he was doing. Being in an institution such as Harvard and being willing to be unconventional, being willing to shake up the dialogue, being willing to have conversations about the way to leverage institutional power into doing things for people in St. Louis. Those were the things I was interested in. Any way that we can add some firepower to what we are doing.

I'm looking to meet and be in partnership and family with people who are taking it that seriously. Those are the people who shift from being an ally to a marcher. Shift from passively chanting "Black Lives Matter" with you to figuring out how they can do something serious for people back home who need material things. People who are going to help you throw some haymakers at the system, while flicking the bird and letting others wonder how the hell you figured out this maneuver. Instead of a person who wants to sit down and have an eighty-dollar steak with you and put you back on a jet.

ML: You both have a passion for history. It is a framework that roots you in whatever you're doing. Why is history so important to you?

TP: The first black history project I worked on was me and my mother making a black history book in first or second grade. I've always had a yearning for history and an understanding that history is important because it connects you to the story of what your people have done. A key part for me of being an activist in St. Louis was learning the history of activism in St. Louis—the Percy Greens and the Ivory Perrys and even people like my grandmother, Josephine Baker, who was one of the first women to desegregate the workforce in the city. She wasn't even trying to be an activist. She was a person who got a job and was trying to go to work. St. Louis has needed a political uprising since its conception.

The number one thing you have to understand is that the mainstream conception of black history in America is a goddamn lie. It says that our greatness started in the bellies of slave ships where people were eating vomit and committing suicide because the voyage was so horrible. Yes, that's a part of our history, but when you understand that the totality of our history is not that, it places us in the context of a different type of greatness. So, when you meet white people who understand that the entirety of black history is not just us being downtrodden and asking the government for shit, it creates a different context for union. Then you can have a relationship that isn't based on pity of my blackness.

ML: What about you, Walt? How does your passion for history relate to activism?

WJ: When I was starting to research the history of St. Louis, I would find things out and want to check: Is this something that is interesting for Tef as an activist? Or is this just antiquarian? I remember sending Tef an email when I found out that Dred Scott was buried a mile, a mile and a half, from where everything started in Ferguson, on the same street, West Florissant Avenue. And Tef's response was, "Wow, that's amazing." I could tell you seven or ten stories like that about uncanny proximities in St. Louis. I still don't have a theoretical analysis of why it seems so powerful, the way these things are so close to one another, but I can say that I have learned so much from the proximity of historical events with present-day events. It's like the city is trying to tell you something.

I'd be embarrassed to tell that story if it hadn't resonated with Tef. When it did, I thought, "Now I understand that this is an interesting way to think because it energized Tef." It gave him a different kind of knowledge, a different kind of tool in his arsenal as he went into battle out there.

I also found out that St. Louis is a place where there had been consequential black–white radical alliances throughout the twentieth century. And I think knowledge of that has direct bearing on the kinds of alliances that can seem possible today.

TP: A present-day misconception about Ferguson, and St. Louis in general, is that black and white people have just never gotten along in St. Louis. Actually, we got along great to some extent. Middle-class and poor white people and black people. Yeah, we have racial tensions and stuff like that, but overall, the media exploited the polarization way more than we did. We had white people at protests. I've got white friends. I've gone to jail with white people.

WJ: On the whole, I think one could say that the history of black St. Louis has been covered up. The history of the greatness of black St. Louis, the history of the radicalism of black St. Louis. Black people are barely memorialized in that city. The amount of black achievement in that city is extraordinary: the number of artistic geniuses, the number of political radicals, the number of great athletes from St. Louis—but you don't see that memorialized in the fabric of the city.

I can't speak for what black people in St. Louis know about the black history of St. Louis, but I can guess that those who know a lot about it have probably had to work pretty hard on their own to find it out.

TP: You're right about that.

WJ: There are major, major events in the history of St. Louis that people don't know. In 1959 they tore down almost 500 acres—*an area about a third of the size of Manhattan*—of black St. Louis called Mill Creek Valley. They tore it down. And basically nothing has happened to Mill Creek Valley since then. They displaced 20,000 people. They assumed the displaced people would find houses. Some went into the Pruitt-Igoe housing project, others just kind of dispersed throughout the city. There was no real plan for their relocation and there was no real plan for the redevelopment of the area.

ML: Tef, we've been talking a lot about history, but can you say something about how you envision the future of activism in St. Louis?

TP: To me the word "activism" is a padded landing for the white progressive intelligentsia. They are scared of revolution; they are scared of the notion that things have to change. Casual activism got us here—the notion that we can take two while you keep three. If we're going to actually be in this, then we're going to divide it equally.

That's part of why I self-identify as a revolutionary. I use any opportunity to introduce that word because I feel that's what is needed. We need a revolution of our mind frame, a revolution of the way we're seeing things, a revolution of the way we love. All of this needs to change. We're all colonized into thinking and feeling certain ways. I'm challenging the notion of those feelings.

ML: What do you think about the concept of the revolutionary, Walt?

WJ: I'm at a university where people talk about revolution all the time without seeming effect, without really knowing how to do it—revolution possesses a kind of weightlessness for so many of us. I was very impressed by the way that Tef takes the idea of revolution and applies it in very practical ways. One of the best examples of this is the Books and Breakfast program that he helped start, based on part of the Black Panther's Ten-Point Program: it's a small-scale community initiative in which folks of all ages are invited to come have free breakfast, take free books about black history and revolutionary thought, and then discuss the ideas as a community. This is such a consequential initiative, not just in terms of how many books it gives out or how many breakfasts it has served, but in terms of trying to figure out a different way to be human. For me, seeing that program in action was life changing. It inspired me to ask: How can I try to replicate this or build on it? How can I imagine a project that's not going to start by trying to change the world as The World—all at once—but do that in a material, immediate, capillary fashion? Just to get going on something tangible and hopefully consequential, and learn the theory along the way. That's been a real revolution for me.

SOLIDARITY THROUGH POETRY

Mark Nowak

(from Social Poetics*)*

THE WORKER WRITERS SCHOOL (WWS) is an experiment in solidarity. Over the past fifteen years, our workshops have created spaces for participants to reimagine their relationship to work, nurtured new literary voices from the global working class, and produced new tactics for social change. WWS workshops have engaged workers in the United States, Canada, Puerto Rico, Panama, South Africa, Belgium, the Netherlands, the United Kingdom, and elsewhere.

WWS seeks to distinguish itself from the short-term engagement sought by most literary workshops, which might only last a week or month at a particular library, school, nursing home, or literary center. By contrast, WWS forms long-term bonds with worker centers and then recruits people from those fields—domestic workers, taxi drivers, fast food restaurant workers, and others—to become part of our ongoing collaborative project. In fall 2019, for example, we are celebrating our ninth year in collaboration with

Domestic Workers United, the group that organized and fought for the first domestic workers' bill of rights ever signed into law.

Who inspired this idea of using poetry workshops to organize social movements and working-class solidarity? *Social Poetics* details what I have taken to calling, borrowing from Howard Zinn, a people's history of the poetry workshop. In the United States, it traces that thread through uprisings that include the Watts rebellion and the New York City teachers' strike of 1968; globally, the scope of this history includes the Sandinista poetry workshops of Ernesto Cardenal and anti-apartheid trade union poetry workshops in South Africa. Even more specifically, WWS has consistently drawn inspiration from the writings of incarcerated individuals who have used poetry to document their political struggles.

One of the key workshops in this "people's history" took place in New York's Attica State Prison. That story begins at another prison, San Quentin, where on August 21, 1971, prison guards killed writer, activist, and Black Panther Party member George Jackson. News spread quickly, inspiring acts of prisoner resistance across the country, which included a silent breakfast fast the following morning at Attica. Heather Ann Thompson's definitive history of the prison uprising, *Blood in the Water* (2016), describes the protestors "wearing a strip of black cloth as an armband" and, "even more unnerving to the officers, no one ate a thing once they sat down in the mess hall." One prisoner described the protest to a corrections officer as a "spiritual sit-in" for Jackson.

Two weeks later, Attica prisoners rebelled in a much larger insurgence, taking control of the prison's D Yard and upward of fifty hostages. On September 13, after four days of failed negotiations with the state, Governor Nelson Rockefeller ordered troops to retake the prison. Rockefeller's mandate caused the death of forty-three prisoners and guards. To lay blame on the prisoners, prison officials initially told journalists that the inmates had slashed the throats of some correctional officers and severed the genitalia of others. But an independent coroner's report later concluded that everyone who died during the prison raid had died from, as the prisoners dubbed it, "a bullet that had the name Rockefeller on it."

Eight months after the rebellion, Celes Tisdale, an assistant professor at Erie Community College in nearby Buffalo, walked into Attica to begin facilitating a poetry workshop at the prison. Tisdale's journal entry from his first workshop at Attica on May 24, 1972, reveals the personal connection that he had to some of his new students at Attica: "The men are coming in now. I recognize some of them from the old days in Willert Park Projects and Smitty's restaurant where I worked during the undergraduate days. They seem happy to see me but are properly restrained (strained?)." In the prison, Tisdale found something quite different from the irrational prisoners the media portrayed. "Their sensitivity and perception were so intense," Tisdale writes, "that each Wednesday night, I came home completely exhausted." Tisdale's workshops, and the writing produced in them, remains instrumental in my own thinking about the model that has grown into the WWS.

Two years after Tisdale's first workshop at Attica, Detroit's Broadside Press published an anthology of the participants' poems, set alongside Tisdale's journal entries, in a book called *Betcha Ain't: Poems from Attica* (1974). Historian Joy James's description of what she calls the "(neo)slave narrative"—a term she borrows from John Edgar Wideman's introduction to Mumia Abu-Jamal's *Live from Death Row* (1995)—is helpful when reading the Attica prison poems. For James, (neo)slave narratives "reflect the languages of master, slave, and abolitionist." From the discrepancies in power and the social tensions between these three subject positions, according to James, imprisoned writers "created the language of the fugitive or incarcerated rebel—the slave, the convict." James believes that "through their narratives, imprisoned writers can function as progressive abolitionists and register as 'people's historians.' . . . These narratives are generally the 'unauthorized' versions of political life."

A single-stanza poem by Brother Amar (George Robert Elie), "Forget?" offers an example of the kind of "unauthorized" history James describes.

> They tell us to forget Golgotha we tread
> scourged with hate because we dared
> to tell the truth of hell
> and how inhuman it is within.

Isaiah Hawkins recounts the bloodiest day of the revolt, September 13, 1970, in his poem "13th of Genocide," while Mshaka (Willie Monroe) chronicles the aftermath of the Attica rebellion in "Formula for Attica Repeats":

> They came tearless
> tremblers,

apologetic grin factories

that breathed Kool

smoke-rings

and state-prepared speeches.

They came

like so many unfeeling fingers

groping without touching

the 43 dead men

who listened . . .

threatening to rise

again . . .

The writers in Tisdale's Attica workshop were becoming, in James's words, "the storytellers of the political histories of the captives *and* their captors," perhaps none with such intensity as John Lee Norris in his poem "Just Another Page (September 13–72)":

A year later

And it's just another page

And the only thing they do right is wrong

And Attica is a maggot-minded black blood sucker

And the only thing they do right is wrong

And another page of history is written in black blood

And old black mamas pay taxes to buy guns that killed their sons

And the consequence of being free . . . is death

And your sympathy and tears always come too late

And the only thing they do right is wrong

And it's just another page.

Long out of print, *Betcha Ain't* has been all but erased from contemporary conversations about twentieth-century poetry, social history, and prison abolition. Even Thompson's *Blood in the Water* makes no mention of it, and it warrants only a passing mention in Melba Joyce Boyd's excellent history of the Broadside Press, *Wrestling with the Muse* (2004). In this, it is hardly alone, and it may principally be a problem of genre: poetry anthologies that stand as documents of radical political moments—other examples include anthologies of poetry from the Watts uprising and the New York City teachers strike—are rarely embraced by historians as valuable primary texts. When the authors are incarcerated people, that bias is exacerbated.

Poet and publisher Joseph Bruchac spent much of his extraordinary career facilitating poetry workshops in prisons and publishing anthologies of imprisoned writers. He published poets from his own workshops and workshops run by others in such quintessential volumes as *Words from the House of the Dead: Prison Writings from Soledad (A Facsimile Version of a book produced INSIDE Soledad Prison and SMUGGLED OUT)* (1974), *The Last Stop: Writing from Comstock Prison* (1974), and *The Light from Another Country: Poetry from American Prisons* (1984). When I asked Bruchac about the critical neglect of the Soledad anthology, he responded: "We did that anthology in a small edition and sold it out within a year. (Though we did charge only $1.50 for it.) People I spoke to directly liked it, were impressed by the sophistication of the work, were surprised because they had preconceptions about inmates being illiterate or not thoughtful enough to be writers. But I do not recall our getting any reviews, so there was little or no 'critical response' to speak of."

The poems in Bruchac's anthologies are passionate and fierce, skillfully crafted and politically astute. In the preface to *Words from the House of the Dead*, the incarcerated authors suggest that their writings "should not be regarded as an attempt at artistic art, but rather as social art." This is a theme echoed throughout all of Bruchac's prison writing anthologies, and it is not a theme imposed by him. Indeed, the first prison writing workshops he ever facilitated started only four months after the Attica uprising and in a nearby prison, where he found that the inmates attending his workshop were also profoundly interested in the potential of poetry as a "social art":

> Half of the men in my workshop were survivors of the massacre that took place at Attica and a number of them were still recovering from gunshot wounds. So they were more than interested in poetry as a societal statement and a mirror of everything that had happened and was still happening to incarcerated men and women. Some of the things they wrote—which I did not publish at the time, quite frankly, to protect them from repercussions from the powers that be—were directly about their experiences during the take-over. . . . My students—who were a varied group ethnically, black, white, Hispanic—were very aware of all that was going on around the country.

In the workshops, Bruchac exposed the students to other politically conscious poetry that spoke to the themes that interested them, and encouraged them to think of it as a space of social solidarity in which they could freely talk and write about their experiences.

Nowak

I made it a point to expose the men in the workshop to a very wide range of poetry, including poems by Amiri, by Etheridge Knight, and many others. I was an editor back then of *BLACK BOX*, a poetry magazine on cassette, and played for them the issue that included my old friend Etheridge reading a number of his poems, including "The Idea of Ancestry." They were galvanized by that. I told them from the start that I would never judge them on the content of what they wrote, only on how effectively they managed to communicate what they wanted to express. I was told many times that when they were in the workshop they did not feel as if they were in prison. They trusted that I saw them not as inmates, but as human beings.

These important volumes by Bruchac and others, nevertheless, have been and continue to be erased from our historical memories, our literary histories, and the very institutions that are meant to safeguard materials such as these. My copy of *Words from the House of the Dead*, formerly the property of Cuyahoga Community College's library before I bought it online, has "WEEDED" stamped in black on its first page. Likewise, my copy of *The Last Stop*, published in 1974, is stamped "WITHDRAWN" from the Reference and Loan Library of the Wisconsin Division for Library Services in Madison. My copy of the important anthology *Folsom Prison: The 52nd State*, published in 1976, is also stamped "WITHDRAWN" from the very same library. It surely is not incidental that these books—which speak so powerfully to issues of police and state violence—all were removed from state-owned libraries in a part of the country suffering an epidemic of police violence against black and brown people. To "weed" and "withdraw" them is a way to destroy the evidence.

For us at the WWS, however, the prison workshops of Tisdale, Bruchac, and others have become essential models for the aesthetic production of people's histories (of the Attica uprising or taxi driver protests in NYC, for example), new working-class resistance literature, verse documentaries about prison conditions across the country, abolitionist manifestoes, and poetry as "social art." In these historical workshops and anthologies, we have discovered ways to create innovative spaces where writing poetry in community with other workers becomes a new form of solidarity—and a new form of insurgency, too.

'ALAMS FROM THE BLACK HORSE PRISON, TRIPOLI, CIRCA 1981

Khaled Mattawa

Author's Note (poems on reverse):
'Alams are short poems composed and chanted by Bedouin poets of eastern Libya and western Egypt. Unrhymed short phrases, 'alams are pithy statements often quoted in daily conversation to express an individual's immediate circumstances. 'Alams are also called *ghinawat* (little songs). For more on the form, see Lila Abu-Lughod's *Veiled Sentiments: Honor and Poetry in a Bedouin Society* (1986).

El-Mufti and Al-Shaltami, a medical doctor and a poet respectively, were political prisoners in the Black Horse prison in Libya in the 1980s. El-Mufti recounts how hearing a radio performance of Henrik Ibsen's *An Enemy of the People* on the BBC was inspirational and sustaining for him. This 'alam sequence honors the friendship between these two poets by imagining El-Mufti translating a speech given by the play's protagonist, Dr. Thomas Stockman, to Al-Shaltami, and Al-Shaltami, who wrote in classical Arabic and Libyan dialect, then turning Stockman's speech into a sequence of 'alams.

barely a man
leaving behind
this forlorn town

when I traveled
memory shielded
a feeble flame

far up north
muddled longings
I wore like a crown

with strangers
I was a lame bird
I dreamt up glory

poor starving creatures
brooding nest-bound
a sign from fate

scattered among rocks
plotting my return
to my native town

home once again
how abide their
blindness and greed

with my brothers
poisoning the ground
toying with people's lives

I'm their enemy now
a self-inflicted crime
by consensus decreed

they want to be rid of me
they'd kill me if they could
my house set ablaze

but must I stay put
is it up to me again
my life a ransom

a prisoner, how long
to fight on, alone
to redeem this ground

Mattawa

"WE CANNOT BE THE SAME AFTER THE SIEGE"

Roderick Ferguson

AT THE BEATRIZ GONZÁLEZ RETROSPECTIVE mounted by Miami's Perez Art Museum (April 19–September 2, 2019), I found myself saying, "This is the art we need." González, now eighty-one, gained international acclaim in the sixties, at a time when few Latin American women artists were praised outside their own countries. Though her work is sometimes associated with the Pop Art movement, its frank political engagement with the period of Colombian history known as La Violencia makes it a peculiar fit within the category. Perez's show was the first large-scale U.S. retrospective of the artist, and the timing felt freighted: González's work stands as a kind of tutorial in what it means to bear witness, steadfastly, to the hard truths of a period, particularly when it is characterized by assaults on taken-for-granted liberties and norms of decency.

Presenting over sixty years of art, the exhibition included González's paintings, prints, drawings, and sculptures. During the earlier period of her work, González used industrial paints—acrylic and enamel—to produce figures that were color-saturated and flattened, techniques that were "purposefully working against sophistication" as a virtue set by Western art and elites. She began her career preoccupied with aesthetics, but when politics in Colombia shifted, her work changed as well. We can see the shift to explicitly political concerns in *Decoración de interiores* (Interior Decoration, 1981), for example, a large installation comprised of two lengthy curtains. Each one is a rendering of a photo of a dinner party that Julio César Turbay Ayala held during his tenure as president of Colombia. The piece depicts the president's guests mingling, laughing, and sipping champagne. One curtain offers the image in bright yellows and greens, and the other portrays the image in brown and white. The party goers, drawn in González's blocky style, convey the free and easy decadence of a society's elite, safely ensconced in the interior of their wealthy homes. The curtains seem heavy, as if they are fit for the task of keeping the outside out, but Turbay and his guests were not as removed as the mood of the image implies.

In fact, Turbay was known not only for his lavish lifestyle and his controlled and cultivated media image. He was also notorious for his subjugation of leftists, instituting a security statute that increased the military's powers to detain, interrogate, and torture. The merriment of the partygoers indicates less a life free of everyday cares than their "right to be unencumbered"—as the theorist Jodi Melamed puts it—by the woes that they and their class have inflicted on others. The brown and white curtain, with its palette reminiscent of the original newspaper image on which González based both works, suggests the complicity of the Colombian media in helping Turbay curate his glamorous image while concealing the violence that his administration enacted. Devoid of the festive colors of the other curtain, it depict the elites as bloodless and apparitional, damned by their contempt for their fellow Colombians.

Colombia's La Violencia crescendoed in the 1985 massacre at Bogotá's Palace of Justice. The leftist group M-19 seized the building and held the magistrates and civilians hostage. The government, presided over by Turbay's successor, Belisario Betancur, stormed the building, killing the magistrates and civilians along with the guerillas. Close to ninety-eight people died in the slaughter. The massacre compelled González to decisively move away from what she referred to as "pictorial games" and toward life as a "political artist." Discussing the massacre as if it were a moment at a crossroads, she said, "As Columbians we cannot be the same after the siege of the Palace of Justice."

González's response to the massacre can be seen in two oil paintings, each one entitled *Sr. Presidente qué honor estar con usted en este momento histórico* (Mr. President, What an Honor to be with You at This Historic Moment). The first painting, created in 1986, uses muted greens, yellows, grays, and blacks to depict Betancur at a conference table surrounded by government officials. He is reading a paper with a pleasant smile on his face, and the ministers have donned business-like expressions. Breaking the meeting's normalcy is a man's charred body, lying in the center of the table. The second painting, created a year after, displays a similar scene, but this time González has used vibrant reds, greens, yellows, blues, and purples to depict it. Military officers have joined this meeting, and González has substituted a floral arrangement for the corpse. Noting the contrast between the two pieces, Tobias Ostrander writes, "A symbol of decorum, protocol, and, importantly here, official taste, the flowers transform into a symbol of hypocrisy, a vulgar veneer of normalcy or even elegance that covers cruelty and injustice."

While viewing González's work, I kept thinking about her compatriot Doris Salcedo. Salcedo belongs to a younger generation of Colombian artists, who mainly work in installation but who, like their senior colleague, use art to ally with the marginalized and the violated. Describing her work and the central role that memory plays in it, Salcedo said: "As an artist who works with memory, I confront past events whose memory has purposefully been effaced, in which the objects that bear the traces of violence have been destroyed in order to impose oblivion." She went on to say that her work aims to turn "intentional oblivion . . . into a 'still here,' into a presence."

In an untitled installation for the 2003 Istanbul Biennial, Salcedo filled the space between two abandoned buildings with 1,550 chairs carefully piled to give the appearance of disarray. The neighborhood was a site where both Greek and Jewish residents had been forced to leave the city, and in some cases their homes and businesses had been destroyed, never to be replaced. In one such gap, Salcedo created a kind of temporary architecture to literalize this loss. The chairs recalled histories of expulsion and extermination, histories in which bodies were systematically piled up and thrown out. Through this interplay of chaos and organization, Salcedo observed something about the nature of social violence, that it is—in her words—"thought out and planned with coldness." The chairs captured—to use philosopher

Ferguson

Jason Stanley's words—"the ideological structure of fascism, that each mechanism of fascist politics tends to build on others." Resting between the two buildings, the mass of chairs rendered what was "no longer here" into a presence that must be reckoned with, a presence whose absence has to be observed as the accumulation—rather than the singularity—of violence. This reckoning is part of the practice and tradition of the ally.

In 2007 Salcedo and her team constructed another piece to confront not only the troubles of the past but also those of the present. That piece, installed at London's Tate Modern, was called *Shibboleth*. The title comes from a story in the Bible in which two closely related people are at war with one another. One tribe's dialect does not contain the "sh-" sound, so the other tribe uses their inability to pronounce the word "shibboleth" as a means to identify them for slaughter. From this story, the word "shibboleth" has come to mean any arbitrary sign which marks a people as other than oneself.

For the installation, Salcedo and her team split the floor of the Tate's Turbine Hall in two, producing a wandering crack that measured 548 feet in length. For Salcedo, the installation stood as a critique of all those who are maligned and killed because of their difference. In particular, the crack stood for Salcedo as a border, to memorialize those who die crossing territories not only because of the perils of the journey but because of the contempt for who they are. As part of her agreement with the Tate, Salcedo insisted that at the end of the exhibition, the crack could be filled but never completely erased. "I think every time a violent event happens there is a scar," she said. "I think it's a very important part of the work that this wound remains, this memory of the event remains, because still there are immigrants dying every day crossing into Europe."

In our encounter with the scar, we must recognize history's lacerations and then use that recognition not as a token observation but as a catalyst for action and involvement. True recognition must go beyond mere contemplation. As Salcedo says, "To think a specific reality is no longer to contemplate it, but to commit oneself to it, as the philosopher Emmanuel Levinas wrote: 'To be engulfed by that which one thinks, to be involved, this is the dramatic event of being-in-the-world.'" The willingness to be engulfed by the other's struggle is a quintessential part of the ally's custom. In the context of racism and xenophobia against migrants and refugees, the ally's identifications and concerns are not determined by the ally's citizenship or the other's. The limits of national identity and interests are precisely what the ally intends to transcend.

Not long after I saw the González retrospective, Toni Morrison passed away. In my mind González, Salcedo, and Morrison are linked through the question of what it means to be a witness and an agent. While Morrison was hailed as a great American novelist, she was also a keen and worried observer of fascist elements in this country and others. Those observations can be seen in several of her essays, where the global stakes of her work are clearest. In her 1993 Nobel lecture, she addressed the ways that language can be misused for oppression:

> Whether it is obscuring state language or the faux language of mind-less media; whether it is the proud but calcified language of the academy or the commodity-driven language of science; whether it is the malign language of law-without-ethics, or language designed for

the estrangement of minorities, hiding its racist plunder in its literary cheek—it must be rejected, altered, and exposed.

A year later, Morrison delivered the convocation address at Howard University, where she noted the ways black people—and black women in particular—were framed as cultural pathogens internal to the nation. She considered how that construction was but one example of the series of steps needed for "a final solution": "Construct an internal enemy, as both focus and diversion," she said. "Criminalize the enemy. Then prepare, budget for, and rationalize the building of holding arenas for the enemy—especially the males and absolutely its children." Too astute to argue that only one type of government or political party is vulnerable to fascism, she went on to say, "the genius of fascism is that any political structure can host the virus and virtually any developed country can be a suitable home. Fascism talks ideology, but it is really just marketing—marketing for power." And in a 2002 address at Oxford entitled "War Talk," she expanded her discussion about how the machinery of global capital depends upon and exacerbates perceived differences: "The chameleon -like characteristic of global economy provokes the defense of the local and raises newer questions of foreignness—a foreignness that suggests intimacy rather than distance (Is he my neighbor?) and a deep personal discomfort with our own sense of belonging (Is he us? Am I the foreigner?)."

Like González and Salcedo, Morrison asks us to consider the work that we are called to do in those moments when our world surrenders to the predations of fascism. Each artist, in her own way, bends her art to the circumstances of the other to ensure that an engagement takes place. Theorizing that practice, Salcedo argues, "Art speaks to the other; it addresses an other, an altogether other, even if it does not reach the person it is addressing. The main issue, as Derrida observes, 'is that address takes place, even in the absence of a witness.'" The true ally is the one who, like Salcedo's artist, knows that to be an ally is to live according to an aspiration and with a sense of urgency.

Talking about the urgency of her own aspirations, González said: "I decided to become a political artist because I believed artists could not remain silent in front of such a situation. Taking that position was a deliberate choice." By extension, allies are made out of such deliberations, ones that involve seeing the other's cause as motivation for humanely being-in-the-world in ways that we never were before.

ALLY: FROM NOUN TO VERB

Vijay Iyer interviewed by Robin D. G. Kelley

PIANIST, COMPOSER, SCHOLAR, public intellectual, and artist, Vijay Iyer is a recipient of a MacArthur genius grant and is the Franklin D. and Florence Rosenblatt Professor of the Arts at Harvard University. His work is deeply rooted in black musical traditions, though he also draws on his South Asian heritage, European concert music, experimentalism, and an array of influences across time and space. In the course of twenty-five years, Iyer has put out at least twenty-one albums as a leader, most recently *Mutations* (with a string quartet), a trio recording titled *Break Stuff*, duo recordings with trumpeter Wadada Leo Smith (*A Cosmic Rhythm with Each Stroke*) and pianist Craig Taborn (*The Transitory Poems*), and *Far From Over* with his sextet.

I first met Vijay in the late 1990s. We were part of the Jazz Study Group, a small assemblage of writers, artists, scholars, and musicians that gathered every couple of months at Columbia University to discuss the music from an interdisciplinary perspective. Vijay certainly stood out, having left California with a PhD in music and cognitive science from the University of California, Berkeley, and a unique musical and political experience as part of the Asian Improv movement founded by pianist Jon Jang and saxophonist Francis Wong, radical musicians anchored in black music, Asian-Pacific diasporic traditions, and a revolutionary commitment to social justice. Vijay brought to the New York music scene an unusual level of innovation and openness, but his refusal to treat music as a set of bounded, discrete cultural traditions, not to mention his name and brown skin, often led critics to listen for "Indianness" in everything he did. But he and many of his contemporaries pushed against all of these boundaries, and they pushed against the racism within the industry that not only pigeonholed artists but limited their ability to make a living.

Vijay came up with the title for the interview to underscore his point that we ought to think of "ally" as a verb, as the action of dismantling systems of oppression. He was also referencing Amiri Baraka's *Blues People* where he wrote that turning "Swing" from "verb to noun" erased the agency and inventiveness of black people, as well as poet Nathaniel Mackey's elaboration on Baraka in his classic 1992 essay, "Other: From Noun to Verb." He sent me the title in a text just minutes after we parted, somewhat in jest. And yet it perfectly encapsulated his approach to life and art: ally is not a distinct social category requiring recognition, it is what you do with others to push back the storm and create space for freedom.

—Robin D. G. Kelley

ROBIN D. G. KELLEY: The word "ally" is often used to identify those who are supportive of other's struggles. What would you say the term means to you, especially in the context of making music?

VIJAY IYER: I've been advising a student—by his own account, a privileged white kid from the South—who's doing a project on Thomas Dorsey and Rosetta Tharpe, who were iconic innovators of gospel music. And he's been having a crisis around, basically, "Who am I in relation to all of this?" My conversations with him have brought me to reflect about how blackness in the arts has a caché: it's cool to seem black, right? I've even noticed that on social media, when I post a photo of myself standing next to a black person—literally any black person—it gets more likes than if I just post a picture of myself. I think many people think I'm cool because of my proximity to blackness—but also *because I'm not actually black*, you know? And that's inextricable from the history of black music in the United States being sold by white companies and appropriated by non-black people, or inhabited in different ways by non-black people, which is this sort of way of managing and selling proximity to blackness without the guilt.

But for me, that just can't be the point, right? That's basically what I told my student: "This has to be about what you're doing for people's liberation, not what are you doing to gain some kind of status or currency." You know, Martin Luther King, Jr.'s famous challenge: What are you doing for others? That's the question I pose to myself in every context. I want my music to actually open a conversation and allow people to imagine a different world than the one we're in. And that's the kind of work that an artist can do, because we're not there to answer questions exactly. We're there to stir something up, and also to offer an alternative to the reality that we're inhabiting.

This summer we were playing at Village Vanguard in Manhattan for a week, and I was thinking about how these venues are rooms in which people from very different backgrounds find themselves thrown together. That's amplified in a historic venue that in its heyday was a room where white people would come listen to black musicians. And maybe feel a little edgy by doing that—I mean, it's called Village Vanguard. But then what's the next step beyond sitting next to it? Or sitting and looking at it? Do you feel mobilized by it? So I try to think about what you are enacting by being together and creating together. And the kind of agency you afford each other, the way you listen to each other. And maybe the diversity that you might represent as an ensemble.

RK: Can you talk about that? What is required to make music in an ensemble and are there political implications to this work? What does it do to you, and for you?

VI: I have learned that being in these kinds of aggregates is implicitly to take up the charge of challenging white dominance. When you look at the history of the music, even music that ostensibly wasn't political was almost always a group of black men making music together. Art Blakey, for example, had a sense of responsibility to nurture young people like himself. That's community work to me, even if it goes by a different name.

I've often found myself in spaces that were basically black spaces. And it often involves a mutual leap of imagination: "OK, I think that's something we can do together." Whatever our differences might be in terms of heritage, and cultural awareness, and age, and all that. There's a sense we're in a certain struggle together. I was in Amiri Baraka's band at the Dodge Poetry Festival when he performed "Somebody Blew Up America," which led to him being stripped of the title of Poet Laureate of New Jersey—or rather, there was no longer going to be a poet laureate in New Jersey because of that. We were literally the only non-white people anywhere. I remember we were hanging out backstage, and when it was time for us to play, Baraka comes around and says, "Okay, all the Negroes and one Indian please report to the stage," just naming the hypervisibility we were all experiencing in that moment.

RK: Do you experience that as allyship, or is it something else?

VI: You know, I am really cautious around words like that: these nouns that become freighted with people's agendas. Because I don't know what somebody wants that word to mean when I say it. I'm the same with the word jazz. It's too many competing agendas around one noun. I think it's more productive to deal in verbs: How do we work together toward a common purpose?

RK: Right. To ally.

VI: Yes. I also think a lot about how I embody certain kinds of historic alliances. Because in much the way that blackness occupies a certain place in the white imagination, South Asian culture was very prominent in the black imagination as well. King is a prime example: he was inspired by tactics that Gandhi cultivated, and that was a huge point of reference for him in the civil rights movement, which then changed the world. The Coltranes also made all these musical gestures to "the East," as it was called. You can probably locate this historically better than I can, but I attribute it in part to the post–World War II black experience of coming home and realizing that you're actually not welcome, and then starting to rethink your investment in all kinds of European culture, including Christianity. So people looked to Islam, or searched for a sense of common cause with the rest of the Third World.

And so a particular brand of allyship emerges out of black people looking outside the West for other examples of how to be. And also realizing that there's a common cause there, a common struggle. But then what are people like me in that context? My parents came to the United States in the mid-sixties from India because of the change in immigration laws that allowed for an influx of people with technical and scientific educations. So that's very different than people who were descended from the enslaved. When people say we're a nation of immigrants, those kinds of important distinctions get elided. That said, we still came from a postcolonial landscape.

RK: The African American–South Asian connection went both ways, too. The Dalit Black Panthers, for example. And I don't think it's an accident that the particular variant of Islam that really took off among musicians was Ahmadiyya movement, which begins with a

South Asian Muslim. I want to go back though to talk about how you've worked with a lot of multiracial formations—early in your career, for example, you were very involved with Asian Improv.

VI: When I was in the Bay Area in the nineties, I encountered that whole community—Francis Wong, John Jiang, Anthony Brown, Miya Masaoka, Mark Izu, Brenda Wong Aoki, Hafez Modirzadeh—and the cultural work they were doing was critical to a particular moment in the trajectory of Asian American identity formation. They were doing a particular kind of work that was centered around community organizing, and music as an aspect of that, and it was part of a communist sensibility, actually. A lot of them were labor organizers, in fact.

The Asian American jazz festival, which Asian Improv organized, gave me some of my first major gigs as a leader. I remember we had this large group that I called Brotherhood of the Diaspora. It was a pan-ethnic kind of thing, based in the idea that we could somehow find a common cause. We could do something together, we could ally around something. That brings us back to the idea of ally as verb, which means it doesn't become an identity. Instead it's a purpose, or a task.

RK: Exactly. A praxis, the application of theory toward changing society. I remember hearing you talk fifteen or twenty years ago about the Creative Musicians Alliance you cofounded with Miya Masaoka, Aaron Stewart, and Reggie Workman. And you were very motivated by this idea of creating a collective, and how a collective might increase collaboration across race and ethnic divisions, which could in turn shape the culture of the music industry to respect difference without defining artists by it. What ended up happening with that organization?

VI: Well, we were a bit scattered and it was in my early years in New York City. It's very difficult to sustain collective sensibility there because the city has a way of forcing you into survival mode. So I think that particular aggregate was one such casualty. We were very inspired by the Association for the Advancement of Creative Musicians and the Black Artists Group, which aimed to uplift innovative work by artists of color. You wouldn't believe how hard it is to find organizations that do that. I mean, jazz is a space in which that supposedly happens, but as we said earlier, jazz is really a space that sells proximity to blackness to white people. And so because of that, it's always this peculiar, fetishistic, fraught dynamic. And that's why people push back on the label "jazz," and initiated this other language of the creative music movement, basically claiming a mobility and artistic self-determination. And it was worse in the late '90s, early 2000s, because artists of color were often expected to perform tradition. No matter who you were, or where you were from, if you weren't white then you had to somehow be a folk musician. Channel the ancient ways of your people, you know? It's like, "Can I comment on modernity just like you all do every damn day? We have something to say about this." The projects that I ended up doing with Mike Ladd were speaking to that. They were about people of color claiming the right to comment on the contemporary predicament.

RK: Have things changed since then?

vi: Well, I think what's changed is that we've done it. We've set out this path that no longer seems extraordinary. It's hard to express how much opposition we faced back then; it was actually like, "What makes you think you belong here?" I still encounter vestiges of that here and there, but I also enjoy a certain freedom because I've done all these things and acquired a certain reputation. So then the responsibility, as Toni Morrison said, is to free someone else.

rk: So what's next for you in terms of your creative projects and your attempts to do the politics of making music?

vi: Well, one intriguing thing that's happened to me in the last ten or fifteen years is that I have acquired a certain profile in the Western classical music world, which is the whitest place. Audiences you encounter there are old, and white, and rich. So I try to use those encounters to literally address the powerful. For example, Columbia University is doing an interdisciplinary project called "The Year of Water" and invited me to present a program at its Miller Theatre, which is an opportunity not often afforded to non-white composers. And so I'm giving the money to Flint. Because this program will be presented to a room of 800 white people and I'll get to say to them, "Look, there's this thing called environmental racism. When we talk about water, we can also think about how resources are unevenly distributed by those in power, and also about how the powerful harm entire populations." That's basically what I feel like I can do in that moment: try to make them feel a certain way that might stay with them.

A REQUEST

Tess Liem

Fix me to your idea of midnight. Meaning,
I'm here if you need me. Tomorrow let's spill
water and let our socks sop it up
as we dance. Other things will be true
by then too. Cutting onions with our eyes closed,
humming to the fridge humming: these are the ways
we will exercise faith. No worry if our
wants want nothing to do with us, we will
sharpen our needs. Say *precise.*
Or is it possible we must ask for things because
we believe, ultimately, in listening?
Sixteen years ago you called me and talked about the future
in a way that scared the shit out of me.
Say *perish the thought.*   How does one do that?
Time aside—the past toppled you unperfect is too close
to say it was. Or tomorrow was a lion's mouth

you would step into. Meaning,

ask something of me.

Like the secondhand of a clock, if you hear it you only hear it. Say *pear.*

Click.   Somewhere I have a picture of a man hidden

behind a picture of a cave. Say *prick.*

The technical term for this is etymology. He was there

meaning something and then he wasn't, meaning slightly

something else. Say *pressure.* Somewhere else a slow metronome tocks.

Another lopsided thought. The somewhere of course

is in the mind, by which I mean my mind and with each long sway,

say *continue.*   Suppose that was all I wanted to say.

If I could decide for you too—where are you right now

I wonder—say *continue.* We must.

CONTRIBUTORS

Amy Sara Carroll is an Assistant Professor of Literary Studies at The New School. She is author of *REMEX: Toward an Art History of the NAFTA Era* and *Fannie + Freddie: The Sentimentality of Post-9/11 Pornography*.

Noel Cheruto's work has appeared in the *Johannesburg Review of Books*, *Kikwetu Journal*, *On the Premises*, and elsewhere. She recently won silver in the Short Story Day Africa contest.

Samuel R. Delany is author of *Times Square Red / Times Square Blue*, the bestselling novel *Dhalgren*, and a book-length autobiographical essay, *The Motion of Light in Water*, which won the Hugo Award.

Amanda DeMarco is a writer and translator of French and German literature and philosophy. She has been the recipient of a year-long writing grant from the city of Berlin, as well as fellowships from Yaddo and MacDowell.

Tananarive Due is the award-winning author of several novels, short story collections, and a civil rights memoir. She teaches in the creative writing MFA program at Antioch University in Los Angeles.

Sagit Emet won the Zeev Prize and the Leah Goldberg Prize for Children's Literature for her novel *Gaia's Dawn*. She is also the author of the adult novel *Days to See*, winner of the 2017 Golden Book Award.

Hazem Fahmy is an MA student in Middle Eastern Studies and Film Studies at the University of Texas at Austin. His chapbook *Red//Jild//Prayer* won the 2017 Diode Editions Contest. He is a Kundiman and Watering Hole Fellow.

JR Fenn has published writing in *Boston Review*, *DIAGRAM*, *Gulf Coast*, *PANK*, and *Versal*, among other places, and lives in western New York.

Roderick A. Ferguson is professor of Women's, Gender, and Sexuality Studies, American Studies, and Ethnicity, Race, and Migration at Yale University.

Suzanne Goldenberg teaches art and gardening, and is an adjunct in Film & Media Studies at Hunter College. She is author of *HELP WANTED* and *GOING PRO*, and hosts the CRUSH reading series at the Woodbine collective in New York.

Rigoberto González, a Guggenheim fellowship recipient, directs the MFA program at Rutgers University-Newark. His memoir *What Drowns the Flowers in Your Mouth* was a finalist for the National Book Critics Circle Award.

C. X. Hua is a poet and artist. She was previously a finalist for the Norman Mailer Award in Poetry. She has been published or is forthcoming in *Narrative, Boulevard,* and *Electric Lit.*

Vijay Iyer, a MacArthur Fellow, is one of the most celebrated jazz pianists working today. He is Franklin D. and Florence Rosenblatt Professor of the Arts at Harvard University.

Walter Johnson, a *Boston Review* contributing editor, is Winthrop Professor of History and Professor of African and African American Studies at Harvard University, where he is also director of the Charles Warren Center for Studies in American History.

Robin D. G. Kelley, Gary B. Nash Professor of American History at UCLA, is author of *Africa Speaks, America Answers: Modern Jazz in Revolutionary Times* and *Freedom Dreams: The Black Radical Imagination.*

Christopher Kempf, a PhD candidate in English at the University of Chicago, is author of *Late in the Empire of Men* and *What Though the Field Be Lost* (forthcoming). He has received an NEA fellowship and a Wallace Stegner Fellowship from Stanford.

Rachel Levitsky is author of *Under the Sun, NEIGHBOR*, a poetic novella called *The Story of My Accident Is Ours*, and numerous chapbooks. She is a founder of Belladonna* Collaborative and teaches writing at Pratt Institute.

Sabrina Helen Li has work published or forthcoming in the *Threepenny Review, Tin House* Online, the *Black Warrior Review*, and the *Los Angeles Review*. She studies English at Harvard College.

Tess Liem's writing has appeared in *Plenitude, Room Magazine, PRISM*, and *Best Canadian Poetry 2018* and *2019*. Her collection *Obits.* was nominated for the Lambda Award for Lesbian Poetry and won the Gerald Lampert Memorial Award.

Mordecai Lyon produced *BeFree.TV* (2008–10), a hip hop miniseries that aired on

TUN, featuring artists Pharoahe Monch, Immortal Technique, and Dead Prez. As a journalist, his work has appeared on ESPN and ABC News.

Khaled Mattawa is the author of five volumes of poetry, most recently *Mare Nostrum*. A MacArthur fellow, he teaches at the University of Michigan and edits *Michigan Quarterly Review*.

Micki McElya, Pulitzer-nominated Professor of History at the University of Connecticut, is author of *Clinging to Mammy: The Faithful Slave in Twentieth-Century America* and *The Politics of Mourning: Death and Honor in Arlington National Cemetery*.

Mark Nowak's books include *Shut Up Shut Down*, *Coal Mountain Elementary*, and *Social Poetics* (forthcoming). He is founding director of the Worker Writers School.

Tef Poe, a cofounder of Hands Up United, was in the streets of Ferguson for more than 300 days. He was the 2017 Nasir Jones Hip Hop Fellow at Harvard. His most recent album is *Black Julian 2*, and he is currently finishing his memoir, *Rebel to America*.

Yaron Regev is a translator and the author of two graphic novels, *Ghosts of Love and Country* and *Descartes' World* (forthcoming), as well as an upcoming YA fantasy series called The Door Behind the Sun.

Meredith Stricker is author of *Tenderness Shore* (National Poetry Series Award) and *anemochore*, for which she was short-listed for the Four Quartets Prize from the Poetry Society of America and the T.S. Eliot Foundation. She codirects visual poetry studio.

Mattilda Bernstein Sycamore's memoir, *The End of San Francisco*, won a Lambda Award, and *Why Are Faggots So Afraid of Faggots?* was an American Library Association Stonewall Honor Book. Her latest novel, *Sketchtasy*, was an NPR Best Book of 2018.

Abdellah Taïa is the author of *Salvation Army*, *Another Morocco*, and *Infidels*. His novel *Le jour du Roi* was awarded the French Prix de Flore. An English translation of his novel *A Country for Dying* is forthcoming from Seven Stories Press.

Sarah Vap's *Viability* was selected for the National Poetry Series. She has received a NEA Fellowship, and was recently the Distinguished Hugo Visiting Writer at the University of Montana. She teaches Poetry and Poetry in Translation at Drew University.